THE BEST OF The MAILBOX® Magazine

The Best The MAILBOX
Kindergarten—Book 2

MW01051606

Departments

3 — **Classroom Displays** Child-centered classroom displays.

19 — **Arts & Crafts for Little Hands** An assortment of seasonal creative projects.

31 — **Getting Your Ducks in a Row** Classroom management tips.

35 — **Learning Centers** Easy-to-make centers for practicing basic skills.

47 — **Wonders Never Cease** Simple science for young children.

67 — **Kindergarten Café** Step-by-step recipes to promote independence in following directions.

87 — **Rhythm & Rhyme Time** Songs, poems, and fingerplays.

93 — **Lighting the Way to Literacy** Early experiences in reading and writing.

97 — **All Together Now** Games, group activities, and circle-time ideas.

101 — **Building Math Skills** Activities that reinforce basic math skills and concepts.

105 — **Our Readers Write** A collection of classroom-tested tips for teachers.

Theme Units

112 — **Make a Splash in Kindergarten**

116 — **Pizza, Please!**

120 — **Thanksgiving Remembered**

126 — **Special You, Special Me!**

132 — **Winter Where You Are**

140 — **First-Class Phonics**

144 — **Rainbow Dragon**

151 — **From Hives to Honey**

158 — **A Tribute to Trees**

162 — **Welcome to the Math-Review Zoo**

170 — **Hooray for the USA!**

174 — **Give a Cheer for the End of the Year!**

Special Features

178 — **There's No Place Like Kindergarten!**

180 — **Happy Birthday to You!**

182 — **Magic Moments**

184 — **Jazzing Up Journals**

186 — **Nifty Nutrition**

188 — **Helping Hands: Making the Most of Classroom Jobs**

190 — **Let's Celebrate!**

About This Book

Packed with loads of our most popular ideas, *The Best of* **The Mailbox® Kindergarten—Book 2** is the perfect resource for energizing your kindergarten classroom! The editors of *The Mailbox®* have compiled the best teacher-tested ideas published in the 1999–2003 issues of the kindergarten magazine to bring you this valuable and timesaving resource. Inside you'll find special thematic units, as well as hundreds of fun and practical ideas featured in our regular departments, including arts and crafts, learning centers, management tips, and skill builders. *The Best of* **The Mailbox® Kindergarten—Book 2** is *the* best resource for a classroom filled with fun and learning!

Managing Editor: Susan Walker
Editor at Large: Diane Badden
Staff Editor: Kimberly A. Brugger
Copy Editors: Tazmen Carlisle, Amy Kirtley-Hill, Karen L. Mayworth, Kristy Parton, Debbie Shoffner, Cathy Edwards Simrell
Art Coordinators: Theresa Lewis Goode, Stuart Smith
Artists: Pam Crane, Theresa Lewis Goode, Clevell Harris, Ivy L. Koonce, Clint Moore, Greg D. Rieves, Rebecca Saunders, Barry Slate, Stuart Smith, Donna K. Teal
The Mailbox® Books.com: Judy P. Wyndham (MANAGER); Jennifer Tipton Bennett (DESIGNER/ARTIST); Karen White (INTERNET COORDINATOR); Paul Fleetwood, Xiaoyun Wu (SYSTEMS)

President, The Mailbox Book Company™: Joseph C. Bucci
Director of Book Planning and Development: Chris Poindexter
Curriculum Director: Karen P. Shelton
Book Development Managers: Cayce Guiliano, Elizabeth H. Lindsay, Thad McLaurin
Editorial Planning: Kimberley Bruck (MANAGER); Debra Liverman, Sharon Murphy, Susan Walker (TEAM LEADERS)
Editorial and Freelance Management: Karen A. Brudnak; Sarah Hamblet, Hope Rodgers (EDITORIAL ASSISTANTS)
Editorial Production: Lisa K. Pitts (TRAFFIC MANAGER); Lynette Dickerson (TYPE SYSTEMS); Mark Rainey (TYPESETTER)
Librarian: Dorothy C. McKinney

www.themailbox.com

CLASSROOM DISPLAYS

Our New "Kinder-garden"!

Kiesha
Tim
Pam
Tina
Kim
Jordan
John
Susie
Jane
Zach
Tony
Amy

Plant this home-school connection in the soil of a brand-new year! Give each child a tagboard flower to take home. Instruct her to glue a photo of herself to the center of the flower and ask her family to work with her to decorate the rest of the flower. Have each child bring her flower back to school. Then glue a stem and leaves to each flower and mount it on a board behind a construction paper picket fence. Look who's in bloom!

Missy DiPonio—Gr. K, Bloomfield Hills, MI

Happy birthday! Use a party-themed border to trim a bright background. Write the birthday song on a piece of chart paper, as shown, and then laminate it. Staple the song, student photos, and balloon cutouts to the board. Write each child's name on a separate sentence strip. On a child's special day, pin his name to the open space in the chart and let the celebration begin.

Beverly Nordin—Gr. K, Sykes Elementary, Jackson, MS

Teamwork is the secret ingredient that creates *and* solves this puzzle! To prepare, cut a large sheet of white poster board into as many pieces as you have children. Label each piece with the name of a different student. Then give each child her piece of the puzzle and invite her to decorate it as she likes. Ask each child to place her decorated piece on a large, flat surface in your puzzle center. During center times, encourage children to put the puzzle together—once, twice, or many times! Then mount the completed puzzle on a poster board frame.

Becky Krapf—Gr. K
Richard Mann Elementary School
Walworth, NY

The More We Get Together,

the Happier We'll Be!

The Princess and the Pea

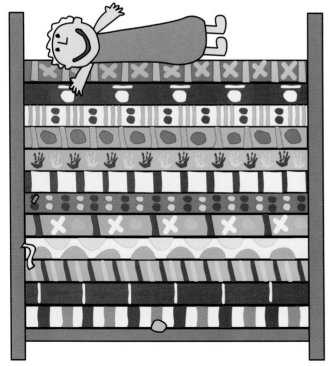

Enhance your fairy-tale unit with this creative display that integrates literature, art, *and* math! After sharing your favorite version of *The Princess and the Pea,* give each child a long strip of bulletin board paper. Instruct the child to paint a pattern of his choice on this paper mattress. Make a bed by using three strips of dark-colored bulletin board paper. Stack and tape each student's mattress above the bed's base. Then invite one student volunteer to paint a princess to rest on the top mattress and another volunteer to make a pea for the bottom mattress. Just perfect!

Valerie Jewell—Gr. K
Chattahoochee Elementary
Duluth, GA

We're Falling for You!

Your classroom will glisten and glimmer with this unique fall tree. To begin, ask children to paint or color a large supply of cardboard tubes brown. Arrange the tubes on a wall to resemble a tree. Title the display as shown. Then invite each child to paint a sheet of paper with colored glitter glue. When the glue is dry, have her cut out a large leaf shape from the paper. Then use a permanent marker to write her name on the leaf. Tape the glittery leaves to the tree for a sparkling fall display! (Tip: Be sure to clean your paintbrushes well after this activity!)

Sheila Crawford—Five-Year-Olds
Kids Kampus
Huntington, IN

Judi Lesnansky
New Hope Academy
Youngstown, OH

These shimmering spiderlings are sure to start your room spinning! Have each child paint a three-ounce cup black (mix in a bit of dishwashing liquid to help the paint stick). Before the paint is dry, have the child sprinkle silver or iridescent glitter on the cup. Finish the spiderling by helping the student add black pipe cleaner legs and two wiggle eyes stickers. Display the new brood on a black background that students have "yarn-painted" to create a weblike effect.

adapted from an idea by June Bass
Cherokee Heights Baptist Day Care
Macon, GA

FALL IS TOO COOL!

This progressive fall scene will keep onlookers checking back weekly to see what's new. To begin, enlist students' help to make a small scarecrow wearing sunglasses. Mount the scarecrow on a bulletin board and add the title "Fall Is Too Cool!" Each week, add students' fall craft projects—such as paper bag jack-o'-lanterns, sponge-painted leaves, or cardboard-tube bats—to create a new look. Finish the scene the last week of October by giving the scarecrow a trick-or-treat bag.

Pam Ingram—Gr. K, Davenport at School, Lenoir, NC

Turkey Dressing

These tricky turkeys will tickle your students' imaginations! For each child, duplicate the turkey pattern (page 17) on tagboard. Have each child team up with his family (at home) to disguise his turkey in hopes of avoiding the turkey's Thanksgiving Day demise. Display each completed turkey; then invite children to guess the identity of each turkey-disguise designer.

Lisa Lucas—Gr. K
Saints Peter and Paul School
Garfield Heights, OH

Display your students' good work in holiday style! Staple a holiday garland around a colorful background. Cut out the title's letters from wrapping paper; then mount them on the board. When a child completes a piece of work that he is particularly proud of, invite him to mount it on the board and add a gift bow. What a pretty sight!

Monica Marino—Special Education, Shady Lane School, Deptford Township, NJ

The weather outside may be frightful, but this board is truly delightful! Have each student glue two white paper doilies on a sheet of blue construction paper to create a snowman. Then have her embellish her snowy friend with craft items, such as sequin eyes, a pipe cleaner nose, and an aquarium-gravel mouth. Set out white paint and cotton swabs, and encourage students to dab paint around their snowmen to create snow. And for an extra special touch, tape a string of white Christmas tree lights around the bulletin board.

Kiva English—Gr. K, Cato-Meridian School, Cato, NY, and Tara Kicklighter—Grs. K–1, Bunnell Elementary School, Bunnell, FL

Use this bulletin board idea to encourage your little ones to curl up with a good book! In advance, take a photograph of each child wrapped in a blanket, holding a teddy bear, and looking at a favorite book. Staple the photos to a bulletin board; then attach a bear and book cutout along with the title shown.

Judy Ruiz—Gr. K, Holaway Elementary, Tucson, AZ

Have each child decorate a paper plate to resemble her face. Then provide her with a hat cutout and a variety of craft items. Program each hat as shown; then help the child complete the sentence. Finally, invite the youngster to use craft items to decorate her hat. Display the faces and hats on a bulletin board adorned with streamers. Happy New Year!

Amy Miller—Gr. K, Community School Age Day Care, Downingtown, PA

Warm up to winter's chill with this friendly bulletin board. Cut two large mittens and arms from bulletin board paper. Staple the pieces to a bulletin board to resemble a pair of outstretched arms and cupped hands. Help each youngster fold and then cut out her own snowflake shape from white paper. Glue the child's photo to the center of her snowflake; then add the snowflake to the board. Finish by writing the title on the mittens as shown.

Elinor Gesink—Gr. K, Sheldon Christian School, Sheldon, IA

Mmm…this display looks delicious! For each child, cut a Hershey's Kisses candy shape from tagboard. Have a child wrap the cutout with aluminum foil. Then have him use permanent markers to decorate the shape with hearts, *X*s and *O*s, or other valentine designs. Have him write his name on a strip of white paper. Then tape the strip to the back of his candy kiss to resemble the paper strip on the real candy. Attach the decorated candies to your wall along with a favorite character and the title shown.

Katie Zuehlke—Gr. K, Bendix Elementary, Annandale, MN

Let's go fly a kite! In advance, take a photo of each child posing as if she were flying a kite. Mount each photo on a background as shown. Invite each child to use art supplies to create a colorful kite. Then help her staple a length of yarn to the back of the kite. Glue the loose end of the yarn to the child's photo; then staple the kite to the board. Whoosh—off it goes!

Leah Taylor—Gr. K, Maranatha Chapel, San Diego, CA

Dive Into a Good Book

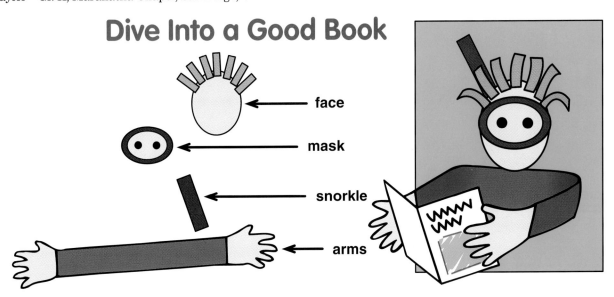

face

mask

snorkle

arms

Why not dive into a good book with this cute display? Have each child cut an oval from an appropriate color of flesh-toned construction paper and then glue on strips of construction paper hair. Next, have him glue on a mask made from a small light blue construction paper oval glued to a larger black construction paper oval. Have each child cut black circle eyes and a snorkel tube. Glue the eyes to the mask and the tube behind the head. Have each youngster trace his hands and then cut out the shapes. Have him glue the shapes to a 3" x 18" strip of paper as shown. Give each child a sheet of white construction paper and have him illustrate the cover of his favorite book. Assemble the pieces as shown and attach them to a sheet of blue construction paper. Display the divers with the title shown.

Johanna Litts—Gr. K, North Central Elementary, Hermansville, MI

Have students brainstorm different springtime animals—such as birds, lambs, or frogs—and then name something each of the animals might see in spring. (For example, a frog might see a lily pad.) Invite each child to make a springtime animal and its corresponding object. Then arrange the animals and objects on a display along with captions similar to the ones shown. It sure looks a lot like spring!

Felice Kestenbaum—Gr. K, Goosehill Primary, Cold Spring Harbor, NY

It's time for bunnies! Invite each child to paint her facial features on a seven-inch circle cut from flesh-toned construction paper. When the paint is dry, have her glue her circle to the center of a nine-inch paper plate. Then instruct the child to cut out bunny ears from white and pink construction paper. Staple the ears to the top rim of the plate. Mount all the personalized bunnies on a board titled " 'Hoppy' Easter!"

Diane Bonica, Tigard-Tualatin School District, Tualatin, OR

Honor your youngsters' mothers or female caregivers with this Mother's Day display. In advance, send home a survey (similar to the one shown) along with a note requesting a photograph. Mount each mother's photo beside her completed survey. Then add student-made flowers and a title to the display. Here's to you, Mom!

Terry Myers—Gr. K
Saints Cosmas and Damian School
Punxsutawney, PA

To create this display, cover the bottom half of a blue background with white paper. Sponge-paint the white paper brown to resemble dirt; then use your finger to draw worm tunnels in the wet paint. Mount paper grass above the dirt. Have each child make a worm by sliding Cheerios onto a pipe cleaner, then bending each end to hold the cereal in place. Mount the worms on the board and add cutout butterflies and flowers as desired.

Pam Ingram & Sandy Ingram—Gr. K, Davenport School, Lenoir, NC

Quiet
as a
Mouse

Need to motivate students to practice quiet-as-a-mouse behavior? Make this display! Duplicate the mouse and cheese patterns on page 18 to make a class supply; then personalize a mouse for each child. Display the mice and cheese slices, along with the title shown. Each time a child demonstrates quiet behavior, invite him to punch a hole in his cheese. When he's earned ten punches, reward him with a stick of string cheese. Yum!

Cathy Peterson—Gr. K
Old Suwanee Christian School
Buford, GA

Celebrate Independence Day with this dazzling display! Have each child paint and cut out her own American flag to put on a bulletin board. Then make fireworks by tracing a child's hand three times on white art paper. Cut out the tracings; then squeeze glue onto the palm and fingers of each cutout. Sprinkle glitter over the glue and shake off the excess. Display the cutouts in clusters to resemble fireworks. Wow!

Conne Opat—Gr. K, Beech Grove Kindergarten Center, Beech Grove, IN

Follow up a reading of Charles Shaw's *It Looked Like Spilt Milk* with this creative display. Cover the top of a bookshelf and the wall space right above the shelf with blue bulletin board paper. Write the title on a piece of white paper that has a scalloped edge and mount it at the top of the display. Have each youngster make a cloud-like form by putting a blob or two of white paint in the middle of a sheet of blue construction paper and then folding the paper to make a symmetrical design. Unfold the paper and cut out the resulting design once the paint is dry. Tape the clouds to the background. Under each child's cloud, write her name and her response to what she imagines her cloud to be. Finish the display by adding empty milk cartons and paper milk "spills."

Michelle Pabon and Lydia Kazakias
P.S. 171 Peter G. Van Alst School
Long Island City, NY

This mouthwatering display will send students on their way to summer! Have each child use craft foam shapes, confetti, sequins, or other craft materials to decorate a construction paper scoop of ice cream. Attach each scoop to a triangle of tan paper, crosshatched to resemble a cone. Display all the ice-cream creations with the title shown.

Michelle LeMaster-Johnson—Grs. K–4/K–5, Windlake Elementary, Milwaukee, WI

The 100 Club

Celebrate the 100th day of school or any counting accomplishments with this display. Photocopy the award (below) for each child. Have each child trace his hands on construction paper. Then have him cut out his hand shapes and color them as desired. Display the cutouts as shown; then use a permanent marker to label each one. (Use extra handcutouts to decorate the title.) As each child achieves a counting accomplishment, fill out an award for him, check the appropriate skill(s), and then mount the award on the display.

M. Lynne Sypher—Gr. K, Brook Avenue School, Bay Shore, NY

Award Pattern Use with "The 100 Club" on this page.

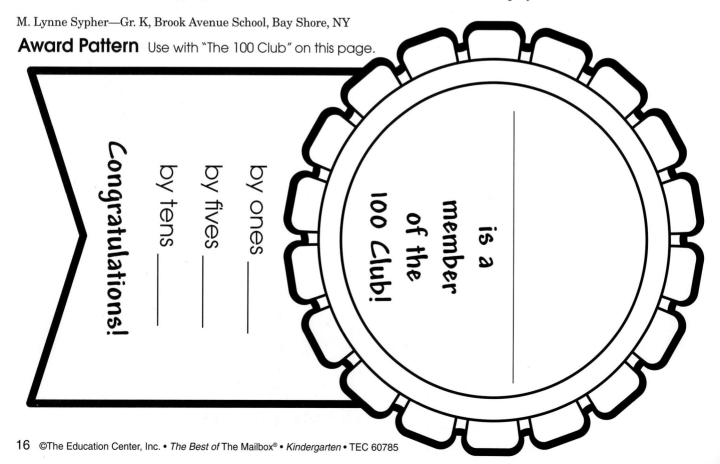

Mouse and Cheese Patterns
Use with "Quiet as a Mouse" on page 14.

Arts & Crafts
for Little Hands

Arts & Crafts
for Little Hands

Johnny Appleseed Hats

Follow up a reading of *Johnny Appleseed Goes A-planting* by Patsy Jensen by making these silvery hats. Provide each youngster with a 7" x 7" piece of tagboard, a 14-inch length of aluminum foil, and a 2½" x 8" piece of black construction paper. Cut a 1½-inch-wide strip of gray construction paper long enough to fit around each child's head and overlap slightly. Then guide each child through the steps below to complete his Johnny Appleseed hat. Hats off to you, Johnny Appleseed!

Directions:
1. Wrap the tagboard square with foil.
2. Cut the black paper into an oval shape to make a handle.
3. Staple the handle to the pot.
4. Staple the headband to the pot
5. Staple the headband to fit the child's head.

Robin Goddard—Gr. K
Mt. Vernon Elementary
St. Petersburg, FL

Shimmering Sharing

These colorful reminders about the importance of sharing are a real catch for your classroom windows! In advance, make several tagboard copies of a fish pattern and cut them out. Then read aloud *The Rainbow Fish* by Marcus Pfister, a uniquely illustrated book about friendship and sharing. Afterward, invite each child to trace a fish pattern onto clear Con-Tact covering and then cut out the tracing. Instruct the child to remove (and discard) the paper backing. Then have her press a small piece of aluminum foil onto her fish to resemble a shiny scale. Next, have each child tear a piece of colorful tissue paper to resemble fish scales. Then encourage the child to share her tissue paper scales with other students, and vice versa, so that everyone has a variety of colors. Then have the child arrange her colorful collection of scales on her cutout until it is completely covered. Have the child use a permanent marker to draw an eye and mouth on her fish. Use clear tape to mount these fish onto your classroom windows for shimmering sharing reminders.

Teresa Shankle, Hospitots Preschool, Johnson City, TN

Foam Stamps

Use foam packing pieces to make this unique artwork. Collect several small plastic lids. Hot-glue packing pieces randomly or in a pattern to the top of each lid. Pour paint in a shallow pan. Invite each child to dip a stamp in the paint and then use both hands to repeatedly press the stamp onto a sheet of paper to make prints. Encourage each youngster to create patterns or pictures with the stamps. Once stamping is complete, blot the stamps with a damp paper towel and store them for later use.

Julie Brown, Wake Forest, NC

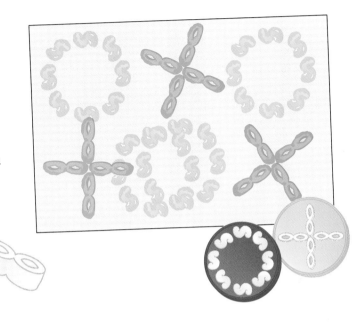

Spicy Apple Pie

'Tis the season for apples! And you know what that means—freshly baked apple pie! Making these crafty versions of the real thing will fill your classroom with that positively pleasing apple-pie aroma. To make one pie, use a mixture of brown and yellow watercolors to paint the back of a paper plate to resemble the top crust of an apple pie. When the paint is dry, use a marker to draw slits in the center of the pie. If desired, add additional details to the crust. Then squeeze a line of glue along each slit and sprinkle on some apple pie spices, such as cinnamon or nutmeg. When the glue is dry, glue the rim of the crust to the front of another paper plate. Display these tempting works of art on a checkered tablecloth and invite children to use them in their dramatic-play activities. Mmm, can't you almost *taste* it?

Deborah Garmon, Groton, CT

21

In a Pile of Leaves

What's the next best thing to rolling in a pile of real fall leaves? Making a picture of yourself doing just that! To prepare for this project, take your little ones on a nature walk and collect a good supply of small fall leaves. Press the leaves between the pages of a book to flatten them for several days. When the leaves are flat and dry, begin the project by gluing a paper circle to a piece of yellow construction paper for each child. Have each youngster decorate her circle to look like her. Then give her several dry leaves to glue around her face. Add the poem shown to each child's project.

Janette Shoemaker—Gr. K
Prairie View School
Oregon, WI

I rake the leaves into a pile,
And then I smile a great big smile!
I jump right in and roll around;
I just love leaves piled on the ground!

Fall Hat

You won't "be-leaf" how cute these hats are! To make one, glue two 3" x 12" brown construction paper strips together end to end to make a headband. Label the front center of the headband "Happy Fall!" Next, staple three brown pipe cleaners to the front center of the headband; then add some masking tape over the staples on the back side to avoid scratching. Have each child select three real fall leaves and then tape one to the top of each pipe cleaner. Next, have each child bend the pipe cleaners in various directions to create a pleasing design. Fit each child's headband around his head and staple the ends in place.

Johanna Litts—Gr. K
North Central Elementary
Hermansville, MI

Holiday Magnets

Patterning practice adds the decorative flair to these versatile holiday magnets. To make one, paint one side of a large craft stick. When the paint is dry, create a festive pattern by arranging plastic confetti pieces. Glue each piece of the pattern onto the craft stick. Then attach a length of magnetic tape to the back of the stick. These magnets make great little gifts or seasonal decorations.

Lori Marie Turk—Pre-K and Gr. K
Most Precious Blood School, Walden, NY

Patch o' Pumpkins

Perch a puffy pumpkin in the pumpkin patch! To make one, trace and cut out two same-size pumpkins from sturdy art paper. Sponge-paint one side of one pumpkin with orange paint. (If abilities permit, provide red and yellow paint and have youngsters mix the colors together to create many different shades of orange to use in their work.) Arrange crumpled tissue paper, newspaper, or plastic grocery bags on the unpainted pumpkin. Then position the painted one over the crumpled material and staple or glue the edges together. Next, glue on a construction paper stem and a large green pumpkin leaf. Then spiral-cut a green circle to resemble a vine and glue it to the back of the pumpkin. Perch these pretty pumpkins in your classroom patch. Just perfect!

Lori Hamernik—Gr. K
Prairie Farm Elementary, Prairie Farm, WI

An Elegant Table

These pretty place settings serve up big helpings of left and right practice as well as patterning and creativity. In advance, cut a large supply of colorful, one-inch construction paper squares. To make a placemat, glue a pattern of colored squares around the perimeter of a large sheet of construction paper. Next, draw or paint your favorite holiday foods on a white paper plate. Glue the plate to the center of the placemat. Fold and staple a napkin on the left side of the plate. Finally, glue a paper or plastic knife and spoon on the right side of the plate, and a fork on the left. Display each child's project on a board titled "A Holiday Table for [number of students in your class]."

Karen Saner—Grs. K–1
Burns Elementary, Burns, KS

A "Spud-tacular" Turkey

Have your little ones waddle on over to the art center to create this printed picture of the big gobbler himself! Cut a potato in half lengthwise and a bell pepper in half crosswise as shown. For the turkey's body, have each child dip the potato into brown paint and make a print in the middle of a large piece of construction paper. Then, for the feathers, have her dip the pepper half into other colors of paint and make prints around the body. When the paint is dry, encourage the child to cut facial features and legs from construction paper and glue them onto her turkey. If desired, laminate the finished prints and use them as placemats.

Kelly Finch—Gr. K
Vaughan Elementary
Powder Springs, GA

Marvelous Mazao

Habari gani? (What's the news?) *Umoja!* (Unity!) If you're celebrating this first principle of Kwanzaa, try your hands at making a *mazao*—a straw basket of fruit—which is the traditional symbol for this principle. To begin, cut out a basket shape from butcher paper. If desired, use a marker to add details to the basket; then glue it to a construction paper background. Next, use a variety of halved and whole fruits and vegetables and colorful paints to make prints on a sheet of art paper. When the paint is dry, cut out each print and glue it "in" the straw basket. Display each child's marvelous mazao during the seven days of Kwanzaa.

adapted from an idea by Carmen Carpenter
Highland Preschool
Raleigh, NC

Oh, Christmas Tree!

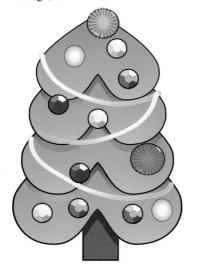

Warm lots of hearts with this shapely tree. In advance, cut out a class supply each of four different-size hearts from green construction paper and a class supply of brown construction paper rectangles. Give a rectangle and one heart of each size to each child. Instruct the child to find the largest heart, turn it upside down, and glue it to one end of the rectangle. Then direct her to find the next largest heart, turn it upside down, and glue it over the point of the first heart. Have her continue in this manner with the other two hearts. To decorate the tree, invite the child to glue on a variety of craft materials, such as pom-poms, foil pieces, sequins, and tissue paper. Or send the trees home and encourage each family to decorate its tree in a special way. Then have them return the trees for a "tree-rific" display.

Carol Ann Bloom
State College, PA

Hedgie's Hat

Follow up a reading of Jan Brett's *The Hat* with this cute craft. Gather the materials listed below. To make a hedgehog, color the center portions of the paper plate halves and a small part of the larger plate's rim brown as shown. Then color the rest of the plates' rims black. Cut slits along the black rims to resemble prickles. Glue the small plate to the larger plate, aligning the cut edges. Then glue a wiggle eye sticker and a pom-pom nose to the brown part of the outer rim.

To make the sock hat, simply cut a sock shape from red paper and use sponge shapes and white paint to print a design on it. Finish the project by stapling the hat onto Hedgie's head. Use the hedgehogs to decorate a wall, or display them together with children's writing about the story.

Materials needed for each child:

9" paper plate half	sponge shapes
6" paper plate half	white tempera paint
black and brown crayons	glue
15 mm wiggle eye sticker	scissors
black pom-pom	access to a stapler
sheet of red construction paper	

Helaine Donnelly and Angela Potzer—Gr. K, Washington School, Plainfield, NJ

Shiny Candle

Light up the holiday season with these shimmering candles! In advance, enlist the help of parents in collecting a class supply of toilet paper tubes. Gather the materials listed below and guide each child through the directions to make a festive candle. These candles really shine brightly!

Materials needed for one candle:
toilet paper tube
piece of aluminum foil
3" square of red tissue paper
6" length of Christmas garland
glue

Directions:
1. Wrap foil around the tube and then tuck the excess into each end.
2. Twist the tissue paper into a flame shape and glue it to one end of the tube.
3. Glue a length of garland around the base of the candle.

Anne M. Cromwell-Gapp—Director
Connecticut Valley Child Care Center
Claremont, NH

What's Your Name, Deer?

Hang onto this versatile reindeer necklace idea! You can adapt it to make holiday nametags, magnets, ornaments, and more! To make a necklace, have a child use a fine-tip marker to write his name and draw a reindeer face—minus the nose—on a wooden craft spoon. Then instruct him to lay the handle of the spoon across the middle of a pipe cleaner (as shown). Have him bend the pipe cleaner around the spoon to create the beginnings of antlers. Next, have him cut a pipe cleaner in half and twist those short pieces onto the antlers. Then instruct each child to glue on a pom-pom nose. Finally, help each child hot-glue the middle of a gold cord length to the back of the spoon.

Joe Appleton—Gr. K, Hillandale School, Durham, NC

Salty Winter Art

Beautiful snow scenes are in your classroom forecast! Provide each student with a 12" x 18" sheet of dark blue construction paper and three to four tree cutouts cut from green construction paper. Have the child use chalk to draw and color a snow drift along the bottom of the paper. Then instruct her to glue the trees to her scene. Have her apply glue with her finger to the snow drift, to the ends of the tree branches, and in various spots in the sky. Next, invite her to sprinkle salt over the glue; then help her shake off the excess. Allow the projects to dry. Display the sparkly scenes on a bulletin board titled "Winter Wonderland!"

adapted from ideas by
Dianne Neumann—Gr. K
F. C. Whiteley School
Hoffman Estates, IL

Ann N. Seal—Gr. K
Verona Jr. High School
Tupelo, MI

Two Liters of Love!

Two-liter soda bottles make inexpensive and sturdy containers for valentines! To make a valentines holder, cut a clean, empty bottle at the top of the label; then remove the label completely. Hot-glue a wide decorative ribbon over the cut edge of the bottle to protect little fingers. Next, punch two holes on opposite sides of the bottle; then thread a ribbon through the holes and tie a knot at each end to make a handle. Now the bottle is ready for a child to decorate with heart-shaped sponges and tempera paint, paint pens, stickers, and glitter glue. Beautiful!

Kristy Helton
Open Arms Ministry
Vienna, MO

A Portrait of George

George Washington, that is! To celebrate Presidents' Day, have youngsters make likeness of the first president!

Materials for one:
head shape cut from skin-toned construction paper (approximately 6" x6")
hat shape cut from blue construction paper (6" across the top)
6" strip of yellow construction paper
black and white construction paper scraps
7 cotton balls
red marker
semicircle cut from blue construction paper (7" on the straight side)
half a round 6" paper doily
glue
scissors

Directions:
1. Glue the hat shape onto the top of the head cutout.
2. Glue the six-inch yellow strip across the hat as shown; then trim the ends to follow the shape of the hat.
3. Cut two small white circles and two smaller black circles from the construction paper scraps. Glue them together to form two eyes; then glue the eyes to the face.
4. Use the marker to draw a nose and mouth.
5. Glue three cotton balls to each side of the face to make George's wig. Pull one cotton ball into two parts and glue these in place to make eyebrows.
6. Glue the doily atop the blue semicircle; then glue this in place below the chin.

Kathleen Rose—Gr. K, Park Falls Elementary, Park Falls, WI

Loopy Leprechaun

These charming leprechauns will bring the luck o' the Irish to your classroom! Make several tagboard hat and face tracers similar to the ones shown. Cut twelve 1" x 9" strips from orange construction paper for each child. Provide each youngster with a half sheet of green construction paper (cut lengthwise), a half sheet of flesh-toned construction paper (cut widthwise), a supply of orange strips, glue, scissors, and markers. Help each youngster follow the directions below to complete his leprechaun friend. Then label the leprechaun with the child's name as shown.

Directions:
1. Trace a hat pattern on green construction paper. Cut it out.
2. Trace a face pattern on flesh-toned construction paper. Cut it out.
3. Glue the hat to the straight edge of the face.
4. Draw a face.
5. Glue the strips along the bottom edge of the face.
6. Wrap each strip around a marker to make a curly beard.

Diane Bonica—Gr. K
Deer Creek School
Tigard, OR

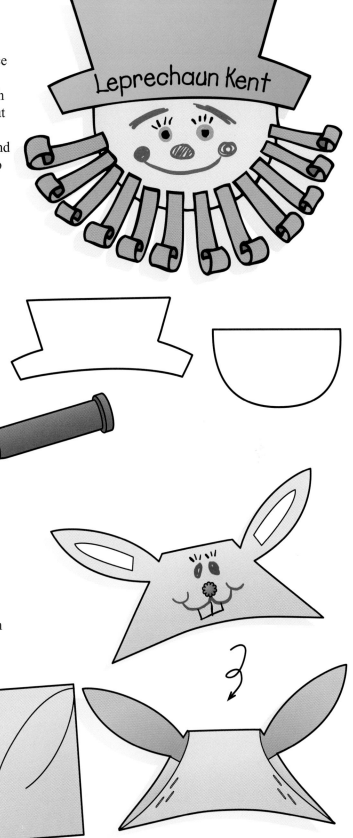

Bunny Hats

The bunny hop will be a necessary activity after your youngsters make these adorable hats! For each child, program a pastel sheet of construction paper as shown. Have each child cut along the black lines. Then instruct her to draw a bunny face below the ears. Have each child glue a half-inch pom-pom to the face for a nose. Then staple each hat as shown. Hippity hop, bunnies are on their way!

Diane Bonica—Gr. K
Deer Creek School
Tigard, OR

Funny Bunny

These cute bunnies will be sure to step into your classroom! To begin, a child glues the rim of a white paper plate to the bottom half of a 12" x 18" sheet of dark construction paper. He glues on a pom-pom nose, pipe cleaner whiskers, and two big wiggle eyes stickers. Next, have the child take off his shoes and socks. Paint the bottoms of both his feet with white tempera paint; then have him make two footprints above the paper plate. When the paint has dried, use a white crayon to make bunny-ear outlines around the footprints. Attach to each bunny a copy of the poem shown; then send the projects home for parents to enjoy!

Diane Bonica—Gr. K
Deer Creek School
Tigard, OR

This little bunny will last for years.
He is so cute, with foot-long ears!

Picket Fences and Flowers

This idea has your budding artists painting a picket masterpiece! To prepare, make several picket fence stencils by gluing together craft sticks as shown. When the glue is dry, place the stencils at a center along with the following: small sponges, flower-shaped sponges, large sheets of white construction paper, and shallow pans of green, pink, yellow, and purple paint.

To make a picket painting, have a child place fence stencils across the bottom half of his paper. Direct him to dip a small sponge into green paint and stencil around and through the fence. Next, have the child use flower-shaped sponges to make pink, yellow, and purple flower prints above the fence. When the paint is dry, invite the child to add a yarn stem and construction paper leaves to each flower. Lovely!

Susan DeRiso
Barrington, RI

Potted Present

Make a mother's day with this unique gift! Have each child sponge-paint a small clay pot. Then help her fill a resealable plastic bag with soil. Place the bag inside the pot along with a packet of flower seeds. Next, wrap clear cellophane around the pot and tie it with a ribbon. What a bloomin' good idea!

Sheryl Spears—Gr. K
Idalia School
Wray, CO

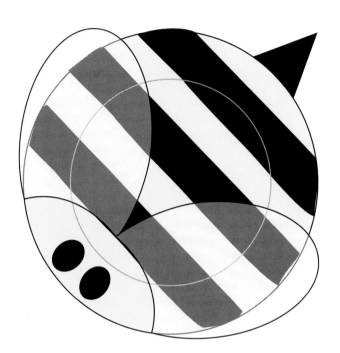

Bees to Behold!

Youngsters will make a beeline to create these cute critters! To make one, paint the back of a small paper plate bright yellow. When the yellow paint is dry, paint on black stripes, plus a curved line for the bee's head. When the black paint is dry, glue two waxed paper wings on top of the bee's body. Then glue a black construction paper stinger to the underside of the bee's body. Complete the bee by gluing on two black paper eyes.

Leanne Gibbons—Grs. K and 1
Boston Public Schools
Mattapan, MA

Splendid Fish Stamps!

Dive into the book *Swimmy* by Leo Lionni with these fabulous fish prints! In advance, collect a class supply of figure eight–shaped foam packing pieces. Cut the end off of each packing piece as shown. Provide students with access to stamp pads with red and black ink. To begin the activity, read *Swimmy* aloud. Then give each child a 12" x 18" sheet of white construction paper and a packing peanut. Instruct the child to draw a large fish on his paper. Next, have him ink a packing piece with red ink and then print fish shapes on his illustration as shown. Instruct each child to use the same process to print his fish's eye with black ink. When the ink is dry, direct each child to cut out his fish and then glue it onto a 12" x 18" sheet of blue construction paper. If desired, invite him to draw or paint other ocean-related items around his fish. This project is sure to make a splash!

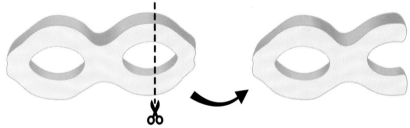

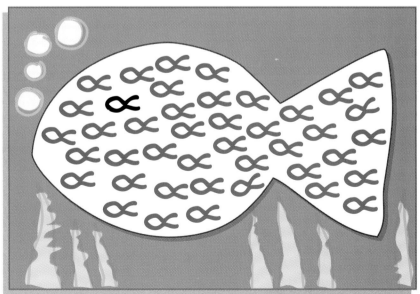

Kim MacMullett, Philadelphia, PA

For "Thumb-body" Special

Say thank you to classroom helpers with this idea for an unforgettable framed photo! To begin, write large letters to spell the words *thank you* on individual sheets of tagboard. Then take a group photo of your students holding the letters to spell the message. Make a 3" x 5" copy of the photo for each helper you wish to thank.

Make a frame for each photo gift by drawing a 3" x 5" rectangle in the center of a 5" x 7" piece of card stock. Write "You Are 'Thumb-body' Special!" on the frame as shown. Then have students add their thumb-prints around the frame. Write each child's name next to her print. Then use double-sided tape to attach a copy of the photo to the center of each rectangle. Thank you!

Jessica Wells, Baker Elementary, Moorestown, NJ

A Fireworks Display!

Create an instant and safe fireworks extravaganza with this simple project! In advance, collect a class supply of empty film canisters; then make a hole in the lid of each one. Cut a large supply of 16-inch curling ribbon lengths in a variety of bright colors. To begin, instruct each child to paint a thin layer of glue on the sides and bottom of a film canister. Then have her lightly sprinkle glitter onto the wet glue. Assist her in pulling several lengths of curling ribbon through the hole in the lid. Knot the ribbons together under the lid. When the glue has dried, have each youngster place the lid on her canister. Take students outside to a large play area and encourage them to throw their fireworks into the air. Oooh! Ahhh!

Andrea Lovejoy—Five-Year-Olds
Park's Edge Preschool
Hales Corners, WI

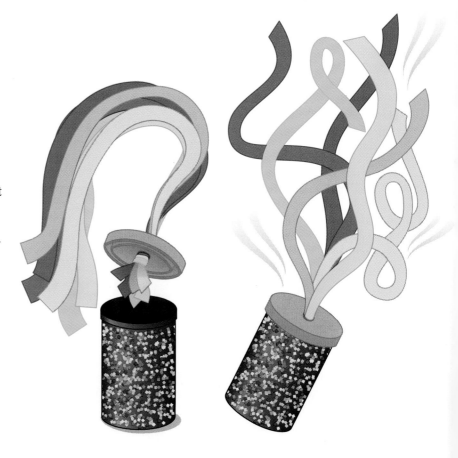

Getting Your Ducks in a Row

Getting Your Ducks in a Row
Management Tips for the Classroom

Pocket That Idea!

Need an easy way of organizing art projects, games, songs, and other activities that go along with your favorite books? Inside the back cover of each book, attach a library pocket. Then, on a 3" x 5" index card, write the activities that go along with that particular book. Add more cards to each pocket as necessary. No more searching for those wonderful literature extensions!

Debra Nerko—Gr. K
Parkway Elementary School
East Meadow, NY

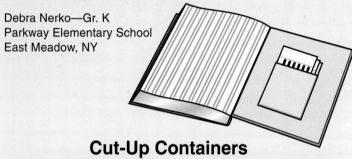

Cut-Up Containers

Many activities have students cutting out multiple pieces, which too often get misplaced and mixed up. Solve this dilemma by giving each child a small, plastic margarine container. Instruct her to put her pieces in the bowl until she's ready to use them. An instant fix!

Lynne Nelson—Gr. K
Sherrills Ford Elementary School
Sherrills Ford, NC

Get Ready for Confetti

Use this idea to strengthen students' fine-motor skills and create colorful fall confetti. To prepare, place several hole punchers and a large plastic container at a table; then stock the center with red, yellow, and orange scraps of paper. Invite each child to hold a hole puncher over the container and punch holes in the scraps of paper. Save the colorful dots, place them at your art center, and have students use them to create festive fall pictures. To keep the confetti flowing throughout the year, change the color of the paper to match the seasons. For example, have students punch holes in white paper to create winter snow. Or have them punch holes in pastel-colored paper to create springtime blossoms. Now there's an idea that packs a lot of punch!

Judi Lesnansky—Title I K–7
New Hope Academy
Youngstown, OH

Feed the Pig

This little pig is perfect for motivating your little ones to pitch in and clean up! To make one, use a utility knife to cut an opening opposite the handle of a clean bleach bottle to represent the pig's mouth as shown. Use masking tape to cover the edges of the opening. Next, paint the bottle pink. When the paint is dry, add eyes, felt ears, a pipe cleaner tail, and spools for feet. During cleanup time, you will hear lots of delightful squeals as one student carries the pig around so that others can pick up bits of scrap to feed the hungry paper-eater!

Karen Saner—Grs. K–1
Burns Elementary
Burns, KS

Hold It!

Booklet projects that take several days to complete can often turn hairy when pages go home prematurely. Solve this dilemma with a stuffed toy mascot. Introduce your mascot to students and explain that he'll be in charge of holding important papers. When a student works on a page that needs to be completed on another day, tell her, "Give it to [mascot's name]." Then the child knows not to take the page home, and she can place it in a designated basket beside the stuffed toy.

Angela Hardiman—Gr. K
Pinson First Baptist Kindergarten
Pinson, AL

Soda Cans at the Easel

Here's an inexpensive alternative to plastic paint cups for your easel. Use soda cans with wide mouths. Simply rinse out the cans and pull the pop-tops completely off. Add a bit of masking tape around each can opening to eliminate any sharp edges. Tape a piece of construction paper around the can to correspond with the paint color you'll be putting inside it. Then half-fill the cans with paint and slip in your favorite brushes!

Kathie Clark—Gr. K
Arrowhead School
Copley, OH

Check In

Here's a quick and easy way to take attendance and help children make the transition from home to school. Create a scene on a sheet of poster board to correlate with the current season, month, or unit of study. Then cut out a related shape for each child and label it with his name. Use self-adhesive Velcro dots on the backs of the cutouts. Add the corresponding dots to the scene. Keep the cutouts in a container near the poster. When each youngster enters the room, have him go directly to the cutouts, find his name, and put it on the scene to check in. Bye, Mom!

Amy Laubis
Kenton, OH

Not Now Necklace

As a group, count out a class set of red lacing beads plus one yellow bead. Explain to students that the red beads represent them and the yellow bead represents you. Students will quickly realize there are many more student beads than teacher beads. Take this opportunity to discuss the importance of not interrupting while you are working with others. Then string the beads, with the yellow bead positioned in the center, on a length of yarn. Tie the yarn ends together to make a necklace to wear when working with an individual or a group of children. If a child interrupts, point to the necklace as a reminder that he should wait until you are finished or try to solve the problem on his own.

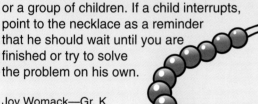

Joy Womack—Gr. K
Maximo Elementary
St. Petersburg, FL

Just Clip It

Try this idea to ensure equal student participation in large-group activities. Write each child's name on a different clothespin; then place the pins in a box. When you need a volunteer, select a clothespin and then clip it to the edge of the box. Once all of the clothespins are chosen and clipped, return them to the box and start again. Now *that's* fair!

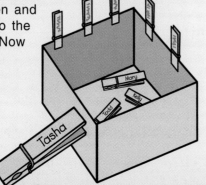

Susan Haemker—Gr. K
John Cline Elementary
Decorah, IA

The Quiet Game

Try this supersimple game to keep youngsters quiet while waiting in line or when you need to speak to a colleague or parent. Choose one child who is standing or sitting quietly to stand in front of the group and be the Quiet Leader. That child then gets to choose someone else who is being quiet and well behaved, and the first Quiet Leader returns to his place. The game continues for as long as necessary, and others will marvel at your group's composure!

Shelly Kidd-Hamlett—Gr. K
Helena Elementary
Timberlake, NC

Cleanup Call

Keep your students focused on the task of cleaning up with this cute call-and-response song. Signal cleanup time by singing the first line of the song. Continue singing until the room is clean and you're ready for your next activity.

Clean Up
(sung to the tune of "The Banana Boat Song/Day-O")

Teacher:	Clean up!
Students:	Clee-ee-ee-ee-ean up!
Teacher:	Clean up your space and check out the floor!
Students:	Clean up our space and check out the floor!
	Clean up our space and check out the floor!

Deb Scala—Gr. K, Mt. Tabor Elementary, Mt. Tabor, NJ

Erase Game

Here's a transition activity that helps students review the alphabet. Randomly write the letters of the alphabet on a chalkboard within students' reach. In turn, give each student the eraser and have her erase the letter that you describe. Give clues such as "I am the first letter of the alphabet," "I am the first letter in the word *apples*," and "I make the sound /a/." After a child has her turn, she may go to a center or begin the next activity.

Rhonda L. Chiles—Gr. K
South Park Elementary
Shawnee Mission, KS

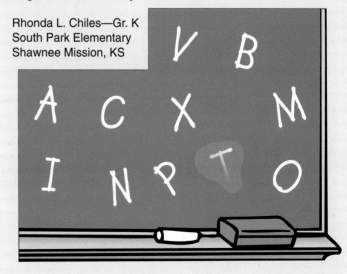

Poetic Organization

Where, oh, where can that poem be? Finding just the right holiday poem or seasonal song is a snap with this organizational tip. In a three-ring binder, place a divider for each month of the school year. Or label file folders in the same manner. Place a copy of each song or poem in the appropriate file. When you need a song to capture the spirit of the season, simply pull one out of the file!

Ericka Lynn Way—Gr. K
Leslie Fox Keyser Elementary
Front Royal, VA

A Handy Book "Dish-play"!

Make picture books easily accessible for little hands by displaying them in a dish-drying rack! Purchase an inexpensive plastic or wire drying rack; then slide a picture book into each slot. Choosing and putting away books has never been easier!

Sherri Woodard—Gr. K
Wayne Grey Elementary
Addison, MI

A Book Review for You!

All it takes is a click and a flash to review a year of class-made books! Lay the class-made books on a table with the titles showing. Then take a photograph of the books. Keep the picture handy as a reminder of the books completed that year and refer to it for future planning. Click! Flash! Finished!

Jennifer Barton—Gr. K
Elizabeth Green School
Glastonbury, CT

Mini Magnetic Boards

Cook up some magnetic fun with this idea! Use burner covers as individual magnetic boards. Place the covers at a center along with magnetic letters or numbers. Then have students use the letters and numbers on the inside of the cover. If desired, use self-adhesive felt to cover the outside of the burner cover and reduce noise. Now that's a hot idea!

Carolyn Parson—Gr. K
Union Valley School
Hutchinson, KS

Pieces for the Flannelboard

Need some new pieces for your flannelboard? Quick, head for your pantry! Use the letters and pictures found on cereal boxes and other food containers. No need to laminate—the pieces are already sturdy. Just cut them out and attach self-adhesive felt or Velcro pieces to the back of each one. How easy is that?

Lydia Davila—Gr. K
Alta Loma Elementary School
San Angelo, TX

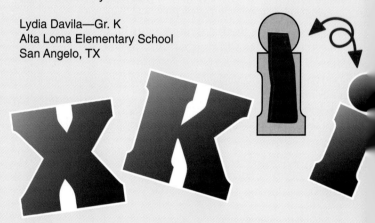

Good-Bye, Glue!

Here is a real timesaver to rid desks and tables of stuck-on glue. Simply spray the surfaces with warm water or cleaner, wait a minute or two, and then use an ice scraper to scrape away the mess. Go dig under your car seat or in the trunk. It's in there somewhere!

Amy Grabowski—Gr. K
St. Odilo School
Berwyn, IL

Learning Centers

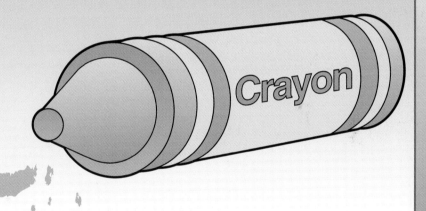

Learning Centers

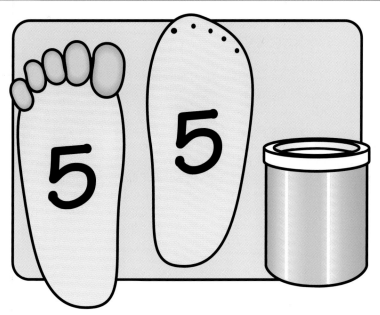

This Little Piggy...

Little ones will get a kick out of this play dough center idea, which reinforces number recognition. Draw six toeless feet on tagboard. Program each foot with a different numeral from 0 to 5. Laminate the feet; then cut them out. Invite your youngsters to create play dough toes and place them on each foot according to the numeral on the cutout. If desired, give your youngsters extra guidance by adding dots to each foot as shown. For added variation, program a right set and a left set of feet in the same manner. Challenge students to find a pair of feet with matching numbers and then to add the correct number of toes to each foot. Now that's how you keep 'em on their toes!

Lisa Nelson, Horizons School—Home Study, Concord, CA

Puzzle People

Clear up the confusion of learning new faces and names with this memorable matching activity. In advance, take a picture of each child and cut a class supply of eight-inch squares from poster board. Glue a different photo onto the top section of each square. Then write the child's name at the bottom of the square. Laminate for durability. Puzzle-cut each square between the picture and the name as shown. (As a variation, puzzle-cut the picture.) Place the puzzle pieces at a center and invite your students to put all their new friends back together again!

Kathy Mosher—Gr. K, Sycamore School, Indianapolis, IN
Tammy Kuehl—Gr. K, St. Paul School, Lake Mills, WI

Just a Dot

Do your new kindergartners need some gluing practice? Try making some dazzling dots to reinforce that just a bit of glue is plenty! First, talk with students about why they only need a small dot of glue for most gluing projects. Have them chant "Not a lot, just a dot!" several times. Then bring out a supply of 1" x 6" construction paper strips. Invite each youngster to make dots of glue on a strip. If any dots turn into puddles, toss the strip and give the child a new one. Reward all those just-right dots of glue with a sprinkle of glitter. Then, when the glue dries, staple the strip around the child's wrist so he may wear it home. If desired, coordinate the paper strip and glitter to match your school colors!

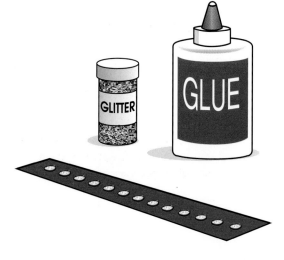

Toni Osterbuhr—Gr. K
Price-Harris School
Wichita, KS

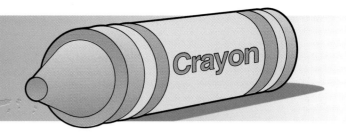

"SSSlide" Into Patterns

Slide in some patterning practice as your youngsters create this slithery snake! Stock a center with various colors of construction paper cut into 2" x 5" strips and a class supply of yarn pieces that are three feet long. Demonstrate how to glue the ends of a paper strip together to form a link. Then review with your students an AB pattern (red, blue, red, blue) and an ABC pattern (red, blue, green, red, blue, green).

To make a snake, each child arranges ten colored links in his chosen pattern on the table and then tapes one end of the yarn inside the last link. Next, he slides the yarn through the remaining links and tapes it inside the first link. Finally, the child adds wiggle eyes stickers and a felt tongue as shown. Invite each student to hold up his wiggly snake and describe its pattern to the class.

Lorrie Hartnett, Tom Green Elementary, Buda, TX

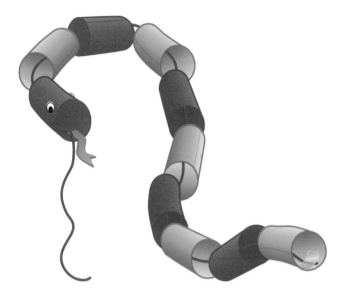

Names in Newsprint

This center idea is just off the press to help students recognize the letters in their names. On a sentence strip or piece of tagboard, use a colored marker to write a child's name in big block letters. Place the name cards in a center along with old newspapers and magazines. Then direct each student to search through the provided materials to find the letters in her name. Have her cut out the letters and glue them on her name card as shown. To add tactile clues, glue yarn around each letter. Show off these newsworthy names by mounting each child's name card and photograph on a bulletin board.

Tracey Quezada—Gr. K, Varnum School, Lowell, MA

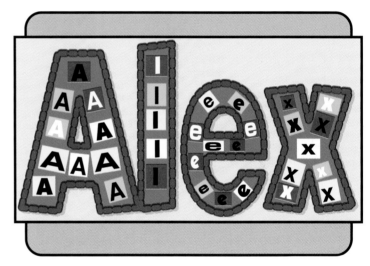

Let Their Fingers Do the Walking

Memorizing phone numbers is fun with this hands-on center! In advance, write each child's name and phone number on a sentence strip or piece of tagboard. Attach magnetic tape to the back of each card; then place the cards in a center along with a tub of magnetic numbers, a cookie sheet, and old telephones. Invite each visitor in this center to place her card on the cookie sheet and arrange the matching magnetic numbers on the card. Afterward, have her practice dialing her phone number on one of the provided telephones.

Karen Bryant, Miller Elementary, Warner Robins, GA

Geometric Jacks

These jack-o'-lanterns treat students to lots of practice with shapes! To prepare, cut several different large pumpkins from orange felt. Then cut out felt accessories (such as hats and bows), leaves, and black felt facial features in a variety of shapes. Store all the felt pieces in a plastic trick-or-treat bucket. Have students work in pairs to create unique pumpkin faces. Instruct one child to create a face and then describe it to his partner. Can she make an identical face on her pumpkin without peeking at his design?

Karen Coldiron—Gr. K
First Kids Preschool and Kindergarten
Somerset, KY

Sounds Good!

Phonics reinforcement will be a real treat with this sweet center activity. In advance, purchase an assortment of brand-name candy such as M&M's candies, Smarties candies, and Milky Way candy bars and several Halloween treat bags. Sort the candy by beginning sounds. Then, for each beginning sound, label a treat bag with the corresponding letter. Place the candy in a seasonal plastic container and set it at a center along with the bags. Invite each child to match each piece of candy with its beginning letter. Then have him place the candy in the appropriate bag. If desired, keep an extra supply of candy handy to reward each little one for a job well done.

Lynda Batalon—Gr. K
Old County Road School
Smithfield, RI

Where Do Vegetables Grow?

Your little gardeners will use a variety of skills with this vegetable investigation. Gather a supply of plastic or real vegetables, such as carrots, potatoes, beets, celery, lettuce, onions, cauliflower, and broccoli. Then place them at a center.

Invite each child to observe the vegetables and sort them into two groups, those that grow *above* ground and those that grow *below* ground. Or for more of a challenge, have each youngster sort the vegetables into groups of *roots, stems,* and *flowers.* Is that some critical thinking beginning to sprout?

Connie Templeton, Huntington Beach, CA

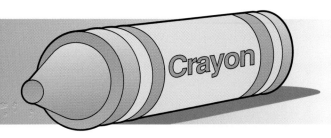

Pecan Pies

This Thanksgiving-themed center will be a hit—you can count on it! To prepare, glue five small foil tart pans to individual squares of tagboard. On each square, write a numeral from 1 to 5 (or from 6 to 10 if you choose). Place the tart-pan squares, some tan play dough, and a bowl of unshelled pecans at the center. Have a child press some play dough into the bottom of each tart pan to make a piecrust. Then have him add the number of pecans to each pie that matches the number on its card. Ahhh…perfect pies!

Jennifer Barton—Gr. K
Newington, CT

Pretty Portraits

Turn your art center into a portrait studio with this "bear-y" good idea. Place a large teddy bear on a stool beside the painting easel. Put a prop box nearby with clothing, accessories, and other items that can be used to dress the bear. Have each child outfit the bear any way she chooses. Then encourage her to paint a portrait of her fuzzy friend. After all the paintings are dry, display them together to create a "grrreat" gallery of fine art.

Wendy Rapson—Gr. K
Kids in Action, Hingham
Hingham, MA

Leafy Names

What's more fun than jumping in a pile of fresh fall leaves? Writing your name with leaves! For each child, pencil her name in the middle of a sheet of poster board. Place the poster boards in your art center along with a collection of colorful leaves and acorns. Invite each student to find her poster board and then glue pieces of the fall foliage onto the letters and the background (similar to illustration shown). When all the projects are finished, mount them on a wall or bulletin board to create a "fallbulous" display!

Shannon Garms, Garland, TX

Gingerbread Play Dough

3/4 cup all-purpose flour
1/2 cup salt
1 1/2 teaspoons powdered alum
1 1/2 teaspoons vegetable oil
1/2 cup boiling water
brown paste food coloring (such
  as Wilton Icing Colors)
1 1/2 teaspoons pumpkin pie spice

In a medium bowl, combine the flour, salt,
and alum. Add the oil and boiling water;
then stir until well blended. Add the spice
and coloring; then knead the dough until
it is smooth. Store the dough in an airtight
container.

Gingerbread People

Youngsters will run, run, as fast as they can to this fine-motor center featuring gingerbread play dough! To prepare, mix up a batch of dough (see recipe on the left) and store it in an airtight cookie tin. Place the tin in a center along with rolling pins, cookie cutters shaped like gingerbread people, spatulas, baking sheets, and a container of buttons and beads. Have each child in the center roll a portion of dough, cut out several cookies, place them on the baking sheet, and decorate them with sequins and pom-poms. At cleanup time, have the child remove all decorations before returning the dough to the tin.

If desired, turn this center into an ornament-making station. When each child has decorated a gingerbread person, place it on a cookie sheet lined with waxed paper. Next, help the child use a drinking straw to make a hole for a hanger. Allow the ornaments to dry overnight. Then turn the ornaments over and let them dry thoroughly for one to two days. Complete each gingerbread ornament by tying on a yarn hanger. Mmm—these adorable ornaments smell good enough to eat (too bad the dough is *not* edible)!

Shirley Gillette—Gr. K, Dorothy Stinson School, Safford, AZ

Santa's Gifts

Santa Claus is coming to town, and he's bringing letter-sound recognition to your students. To prepare this center, fold the bottom portion of a sheet of construction paper upward; then staple the sides to make a pocket. Repeat to make 26 pockets. Decorate the pockets to resemble gifts and then label each one with a different letter as shown. Next, cut out magazine or clip art pictures that have beginning sounds corresponding to each letter. Glue each picture to a separate index card. Store the cards in a gift bag. Mount the pockets within students' reach and then add a Santa Claus character and a title to the display.

To use this center, a child chooses a picture card, identifies the beginning letter and sound, and then places the card in the appropriate pocket. Ho, ho, ho!

Trish Draper—Gr. K, Millarville Community School
Millarville, Alberta, Canada

Help Santa Pack the Presents!

Aa

Bb

Cc

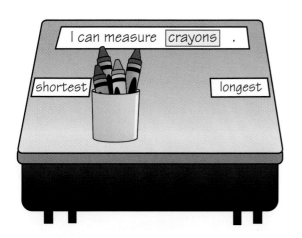

I can measure crayons .

shortest   longest

Measurement Station

Give students ongoing practice with seriation by setting up a measurement station in your math area. Label two sides of a desk or tabletop with the words *shortest* and *longest.* Then program a sentence strip, as shown, inserting the word for whatever items you provide at the center. Place a cupful of pencils, crayons, sticks, carrots, or other items on the desk. Then ask a child to compare the items and line them up on the tabletop from shortest to longest. Keep a list of student names nearby so that each child can check off her name as she visits the station. Change the measurement item weekly to keep student interest high.

Karen Walker—Gr. K
LaCroft Elementary
Liverpool, OH

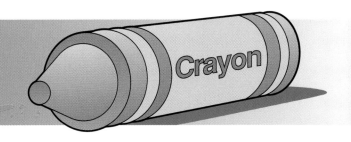

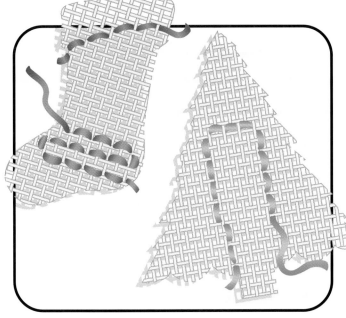

Sewing and Such

Here's a seasonal fine-motor center that strengthens little fingers for writing. Cut out several seasonal shapes—such as a tree, candle, gingerbread man, and wreath—from plastic needlepoint canvas. Then provide lengths of holiday-colored curling ribbon for children to sew and sew and so on.

adapted from an idea by John Barrera
Las Americas Early Childhood Development Center
Houston, TX

That's a Wrap

Use leftover wrapping paper to perfect visual discrimination skills. Cut out a large square of gift wrap that has a pattern of various objects on it. Then, from some of the same wrapping paper, cut out several of the pictured objects. If desired, back the paper square and pieces with construction paper to make them more sturdy; then laminate for durability. To use, a child pairs each individual object to its identical match on the giftwrap square. Anytime games can be made from juvenile birthday gift wrap, or make your center more seasonal by using holiday gift wrap.

Kathy Thomure
Raytown, MO

Shovelin' Snow

Yes, it's that time again! With winter comes the gross-motor task of shoveling snow. Let youngsters in on the work by creating an indoor snow-shoveling center. Provide mounds of foam packing pieces to resemble snow. Then set out several large buckets and a few child-size shovels. Encourage children to visit the center to shovel snow into the buckets. And when the buckets are full? It's time for another snowstorm!

Kathy Lee
Alpharetta, GA

Pretzels, Get Your Pretzels!

Here's a twist for your dramatic-play area—transform it into a pretzel shop! Provide youngsters with aprons, chef's hats, recipe cards, a cash register, order pads, pencils, some empty salt shakers, and a supply of brown rug yarn to twist into pretzel shapes! Invite your kindergartners to role-play making, selling, and buying pretzels. What yummy fun!

Judy Patterson—Preschool and Gr. K
Our Hope Lutheran School, Wayne, IN

Brush Your Molars

This small-group center activity is perfect for Dental Health Month in February! To prepare, gather a supply of small mirrors, toothbrushes, and the bottoms from plastic soda or water bottles (the ones that have indentations, not the smooth ones). Gather a group around a table and give each child a mirror. Ask her to examine her teeth, including the teeth in the back called *molars*. Talk about how these teeth help us to chew. Then put the mirrors away and give each child a toothbrush and a bottle bottom turned upside down to resemble a molar. Explain that students will practice brushing their molars by brushing these giant teeth! Spread a bit of ketchup onto each child's plastic tooth. Then ask her to dip her toothbrush into a container of water and brush the tooth clean. To help with the cleaning, give each child a squirt of toothpaste.

Joy Meyer—Gr. K
Fox Prairie Elementary, Stoughton, WI

Let's Play Reporter!

Present some purposeful writing when you add reporter's forms to your writing center. Create forms for surveying or choosing favorites. Attach each form to a clipboard and invite students to choose an interesting topic. Then have each child get to work interviewing classmates and reporting on the classroom scene!

Julie Pressley—Gr. K
Fletcher Elementary
Fletcher, NC

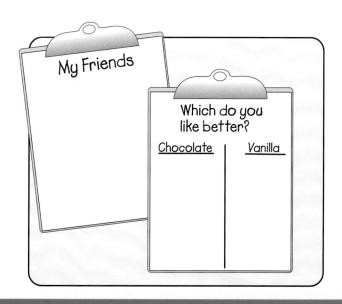

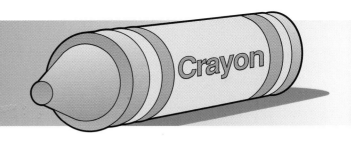

Valentine Memory

Purchase some inexpensive valentines—or save the ones your youngsters give you each year—to create this memory game. Find duplicates among your valentines; then mount each one and its match on separate squares of red construction paper. Laminate the resulting cards for durability. Place the cards in a heart-shaped candy box at your games center. Invite youngsters to shuffle the cards and place them facedown in rows. Have each player take a turn turning over two cards, trying to find a matching pair. If the cards match, he keeps the pair. If the cards don't match, he turns them facedown again. When all the pairs have been found, the player with the most pairs wins!

Suzanne Ward—Junior and Senior Kindergarten
Seneca Unity Public School, Caledonia, Ontario

In Like a Lion, Out Like a Lamb

When the March winds begin to blow, set up this seasonal game to help reinforce a variety of math skills, such as number recognition and one-to-one correspondence. To prepare, cut out and program several construction paper lions and lambs similar to the ones shown. Place them at a center along with yellow pom-poms for lions and white cotton balls for lambs. To play, students each choose a lion or lamb cutout. The first player rolls a die and reads the number. He then uses cotton balls to cover that many circles on his cutout. The game continues until all players have covered all of the circles on their animals.

Sandi Bolze—Gr. K
Verne W. Critz Primary
E. Patchogue, NY

Beanbag Alphabet

This alphabet puzzle is as easy as ABC! To prepare, label each of 26 plain beanbags with a different capital letter. Die-cut letters from craft foam and use hot glue to attach them to the beanbags, or die-cut them from self-adhesive felt and simply stick them in place. Then make an alphabet strip, as shown, so that each beanbag has an identically sized square labeled with a lowercase letter. Have students at this center place the matching beanbag atop each square on the strip.

Elizabeth DeChellis—Gr. K
Victor Mravlag School No. 21
Elizabeth, NJ

A Vowel Search

Youngsters will be on the lookout for vowels in this activity. Stock the literacy center with newspaper, construction paper, highlighters, scissors, and glue. (Be sure to preview the newspaper to make sure there's no inappropriate content.) Instruct each child to cut out several words that are in large print and glue them onto a sheet of paper. Then have him highlight all the vowels he recognizes in the cutouts. Once center time is over, gather the completed papers and have the whole group tally how many of each vowel were found. Do some vowels appear more often than others?

Jacqueline M. Futerman—Gr. K
Pleasant Day Kindergarten, Verona, NJ

Half 'n' Half

If your young mathematicians are ready for some fraction fun, create this math center activity with the help of your die-cutting machine. Die-cut several pairs of symmetrical shapes from construction paper. Cut one of each pair exactly in half. Make a cut in the other shape from each pair, but make sure it creates two unequal pieces. Glue each cut shape to a large index card, leaving a small gap between the pieces. Then use two of the cards to make the headers as shown. Laminate all the cards and then place them in your math center.

When a child visits this center, he sets out the headers, then sorts the shapes cut in half from those not cut in half. Remind youngsters to look for shapes that have two *equal* parts to help them sort the "halves" from the "halve-nots"!

Kaye Sowell—Gr. K, Pelahatchie Elementary School, Brandon, MS

Blooming With Color

Color words are in full bloom here! Program a supply of construction paper stems with different color words. Then set out the corresponding colors of play dough (or colors that can be mixed to make the corresponding colors). Each child who visits this center chooses a stem and then makes a flower that's the matching color. What a bouquet of learning!

adapted from an idea by Kristi Kruft—Gr. K
Mary Walter Elementary, Bealeton, VA

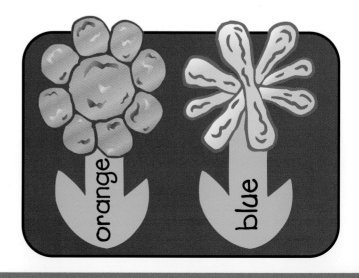

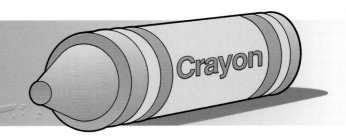

"Sssimple" Sums

Slither into spring with this simple addition game. To prepare, use a permanent marker to draw a snake shape on a piece of laminated poster board. Then draw random lines on the snake to make 11 sections. Write a different number from 2 to 12 on each section. Place the gameboard, oversize dice, and overhead projection markers at the center. To play the game, each child rolls the dice and counts the number of dots that appear. Then he finds the matching number on the snake and colors that section. When all sections are colored, simply wipe the snake clean for another round of play. "Sss-super!"

Kyle Welby—Gr. K, Epstein Hebrew Academy, St. Louis, MO

Hexagons and Honeycombs

Get your kindergartners "buzz-y" with this tracing activity! Provide hexagon-shaped pattern blocks, paper, pencils, and crayons at a center. Have each student trace the pattern blocks over and over to create a honeycomb design on his paper. When the page is full, invite him to draw and color bees in the honeycomb cells.

Connie Collins—Gr. K
Walls Elementary School
Walls, MS

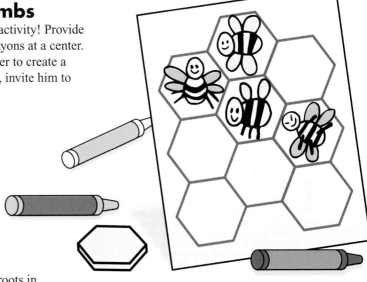

A Growing Greenhouse

These greenhouses will cause youngsters to grow roots in your science center. On a 9" x 12" sheet of tagboard, prepare a simple house template with a large window cut out of its center. Have each child fold a 12" x 18" sheet of green construction paper in half. Help the child trace the house template onto his paper, positioning the roof along the fold. Instruct the child to cut along the house outline through both thicknesses of paper and then cut out the window only through the top sheet. If desired, encourage the child to decorate his house and label it with his name. Provide each child with a quart-size resealable plastic bag, a damp paper towel, and three lima beans. Have him fold the paper towel and put it in his bag. Then have him place the lima beans between the towel and the bag. Seal the bag and staple it to the bottom house shape so that the seeds show through the window. Encourage each child to draw pictures and record the daily changes happening in his greenhouse in a science journal. There's a lot of learning sprouting up!

Brenda S. Beard—Gr. K, Greenbrier Elementary, Greenbrier, TN

Picnic Grocery List

Who doesn't love going on a picnic in warm weather? Encourage young writers to prepare lists of what they'd like to take on a picnic! Stock your writing center with local grocery store flyers, pencils, and paper cut into long rectangles. Invite each child at this center to peruse the flyers, choose picnic items, and copy them down to make a list. Mmm! Let's eat!

Judi Lesnansky—Title I
New Hope Academy
Youngstown, OH

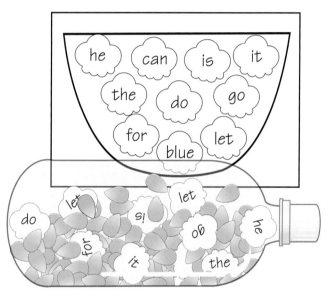

Popcorn Words

Here's a twist on discovery bottles that will have your students popping with excitement about sight words! Fill a completely dry soda bottle about three-fourths full with popcorn kernels. Sketch a popcorn bag or a large bowl on a sheet of paper. Next, cut out several small, puffy popcorn shapes from white craft foam. Label each one with a sight word; then slip them into the bottle. Tightly secure the bottle top and give the bottle a shake! Write all the words you've hidden in the bottle on the bag or bowl. Duplicate the list; then put the copies in your reading center along with the bottle of popcorn words. Ask a child at the center to locate words and then highlight each one she finds on a copy of the list.

As a variation, write the words on simple rectangles or on other shapes and fill the bottle with sand, salt, rice, or another filler.

Jo Montgomery—PreK and Gr. K, John C. French Elementary
Cuero, TX

The Scoop on Patterning

The weather's just right for some cool ice-cream math! To prepare this center activity, draw a large ice-cream cone on a 12" x 18" sheet of construction paper. Then cut some scoops of ice cream (sized to fit the cone) from various colors of construction paper. Make patterning cards by drawing ice-cream cones with various scoop color patterns on index cards. Laminate the cone, the scoops, and the patterning cards for durability. Then slip the scoops and cards into a two-pocket folder for easy storage. A child at this center chooses a patterning card, then creates the matching pattern with the large scoops and cone. Before you know it, little ones will have patterning practice licked!

Lisa Mascheri—Exceptional Education, Midway Elementary, Sanford, FL

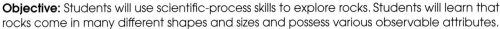

Wonders Never Cease

Simple Science for Young Children

C'mon, Everybody, Let's Rock!

Did you know that everybody lives on a rock? That's because rocks cover the whole earth! Use the ideas in this unit to get students exploring this form of matter that is all around us. C'mon, everybody!

ideas by Susan A. DeRiso and Lynn C. Mode

Objective: Students will use scientific-process skills to explore rocks. Students will learn that rocks come in many different shapes and sizes and possess various observable attributes.

Safety: Safety goggles should be worn during all activities in which there is any potential for liquids or solids to accidentally get into the eyes.

Collecting data

Getting Ready for Rocks

Enlist the help of your little rock hounds to gather the main ingredients of this unit! Give each child a paper lunch bag to take home. Ask him to search for an assortment of different rocks. Encourage children to look in places such as their backyards, schoolyards, parks, or even gardening shops (with permission). Have each child bring his bag of rocks back to school and you're ready to rock on!

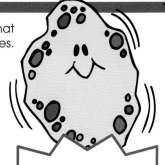

Did You Know?
People collect all sorts of different things. But rocks are the *oldest* things a person can collect!

Observing
Communicating
Defining

Discovery!

Please do not disturb—young petrologists are hard at work in this discovery center! To prepare the center, provide a tub of water, a few toothbrushes, paper towels, and a pencil. (Also have a sheet of chart paper and a marker nearby for you.) When a child visits this center, have her write her name on a paper towel. Then invite her to dip her rocks in the water, scrub them with a toothbrush, and put them on her labeled towel. As children verbalize their discoveries, write them on the chart paper. What wonderful rock discoveries!

Did You Know?
A person who studies rocks is called a *petrologist.* Gee! Maybe that's for me!

Observing
Communicating
Defining

Can We Talk?

Youngsters will uncover vocabulary galore in just a little conversation about rocks! After each child has had a chance to clean and study his rocks (in "Discovery!"), gather your students in view of the rocks and the chart that you started during that activity. Review the words already on the chart. Then invite students to look at and handle the dry rocks. Encourage children to describe what they notice; then record their responses on the chart, adding picture cues as desired. Wow—that's a load of language!

shiny	square
not shiny	oval
small	stripy
bumpy	scratchy
speckled	round

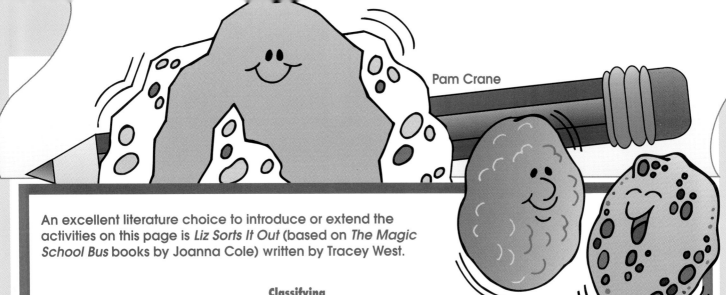

Pam Crane

An excellent literature choice to introduce or extend the activities on this page is *Liz Sorts It Out* (based on *The Magic School Bus* books by Joanna Cole) written by Tracey West.

Classifying
Communicating
Predicting
Counting

Sorting It Out

All hands are definitely *on* in this sorting activity! In advance, gather a supply of blank index cards and yarn circles. Then read the words on the chart (made in "Can We Talk?"). Ask children to predict which word applies to the most rocks. Write their responses on the board. Then ask each child in a small group to pick up a rock (in turn) and choose the word that best describes it. Cut out the word she refers to (from the chart) and place it inside one of the yarn circles. Then have the child put her rock inside that circle. Repeat the process until all the rocks have been sorted. Ask different children to count the rocks in the circles and record the numbers on index cards. Place each number card near its corresponding circle. Discuss the results. (Don't dismantle the sorted collection just yet! You'll need it for "Same *and* Different.")

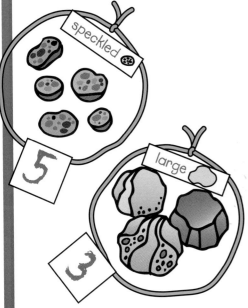

Classifying
Justifying decisions

Same *and* Different

Securely fasten all thinking caps for this mind-expanding activity! Refer your students to the sorting circles from "Sorting It Out." Ask children if any of the rocks could go in more than one circle. For example, is there a *small* rock that is also *bumpy*? If so, show students how to overlap the edges of the two circles and place the rock in the middle (as in a Venn diagram). After introducing this activity, keep it available for a science center activity. The possibilities go on and on!

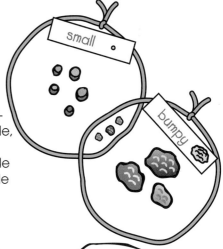

Extension Activities

• Extend the use of the sorted rock collection by making a floor bar graph. Use the labels from the circles to designate each column. The rest is up to the kids!

• For fun and creativity, provide a variety of art supplies and invite each child to decorate one rock to be his *pet rock.*

• Encourage children to explore the different hardnesses of the rocks by scraping several of them with a penny. Which rocks are harder than a penny? Softer than a penny? Another opportunity for classification!

Literature Links

Milo and the Magical Stones by Marcus Pfister
My Ol' Man by Patricia Polacco
On My Beach There Are Many Pebbles by Leo Lionni

Wonders Never Cease

Simple Science for Young Children

Let the Water Out!

Parched for some simple science fun? These hands-on activities about dehydration are bubbling over with science discovery opportunities.

ideas by Suzanne Moore

Objective: Students will predict, observe, and record changes in foods that do and do not have water in them.

Vocabulary: dehydration

Is It Soup Yet?

Soup's on! Or is it? In this activity, your little ones will discover for themselves the very important missing ingredient. Gather your children around; then empty four or five packets of dried soup mix into a large pot. (Adjust the number of packets needed according to the number of children in your class.) Then pass the pot around with a ladle in it. Ask your students if they'd like some soup. When you're met with their quizzical looks of disbelief, prompt youngsters to explain that the powder isn't soup yet. Guide them to determine the need for water. Then prepare the soup according to the package directions. As children sample the prepared soup, discuss the differences between the soup with and without water. *Now* it's soup!

Did You Know?
The powdered soup mix was *dehydrated.* That means that all the water was taken out of it.

Defrosted	Dried
feels mushy	feels hard
green	white
bigger	smaller
same shape	same shape
drippy	no water

Bean vs. Bean

Bean goes up against bean to give your students firsthand experience with dehydration concepts. You will need a bag of dried lima beans, a bag of frozen lima beans (thawed), a lima bean chart similar to the one shown, magnifying lenses, and a plastic plate for each child. Give each child a plate and ask her to take a few of each type of lima bean. Then encourage her to carefully examine each type of bean. Do the beans look the same? Feel the same? How are they alike and different? Are they ready to eat? Write student responses on the lima bean chart and discuss the results. Guide students to determine that the dried beans do not have water in them. Collect all beans at the end of your investigation.

Put That Back!

Ask your students if they think they can somehow get the water back into the dried lima beans. After discussing their ideas, immerse a handful of dried lima beans in a cup of water. Let them sit overnight and look for the results in the morning!

Go Bananas!

Add a little graphing practice to your dehydration explorations with this banana activity. In advance, duplicate a yellow banana (page 52) for each child. Draw a two-column graph on chart paper. Title one column "fresh" and the other column "dehydrated." Then display a bunch of bananas and a bag of unlabeled banana chips. Ask your students to visually compare them, guiding students to state that the banana chips have been dehydrated. Then give each small group of children a couple of bananas, banana chips, and plastic knives. Ask each group member to use his senses to examine the bananas. Then give each child a banana cutout. Have him write his name on the cutout and post it on the chart to indicate which type of banana he likes best.

fresh	dehydrated
Sue	
Kim	Paul
Eric	Beth
Keith	Griffin

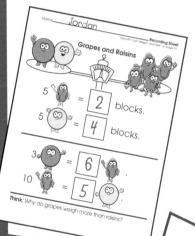

Just "Weight" and See

Mmmm—who doesn't love a big juicy bunch of grapes! Give each child a grape or two, prompting youngsters to note how juicy each grape is. What makes the juice? What would happen if the water was dried out of the grapes? Raisins!

After this introduction, arrange in a center a bunch of grapes, some raisins, a balance scale, one-inch blocks, and a class supply of the recording sheet on page 53. Encourage children to freely explore the weights of the grapes and raisins. Then guide them to complete page 53. Why do the raisins weigh so much less?

Did You Know?

Raisins are made from seedless grapes. When the grapes are ripe, workers pick them and let them dry on clean paper trays next to the grapevines. The sun dries the grapes in about two to three weeks. It takes more than four pounds of grapes to make one pound of raisins!

Apple Leather

Culminate your study of dehydration with this sweet and chewy snack. Line a baking sheet with plastic wrap. Tint two cups of smooth applesauce with red coloring; then spread it thinly on the wrap. Ask your children to predict what will happen if you put the applesauce in a warm oven for several hours. Jot down their ideas; then find out! Bake the applesauce at 150° for six to eight hours. Remove the sheet when the applesauce looks like leather. While it cools, invite students to take a peek and discuss what they observe. When it is cool, peel the wrap off the leather. Roll it up; then cut it into bite-sized pieces. Tasty samples of science!

Banana Patterns
Use with "Go Bananas!" on page 51.

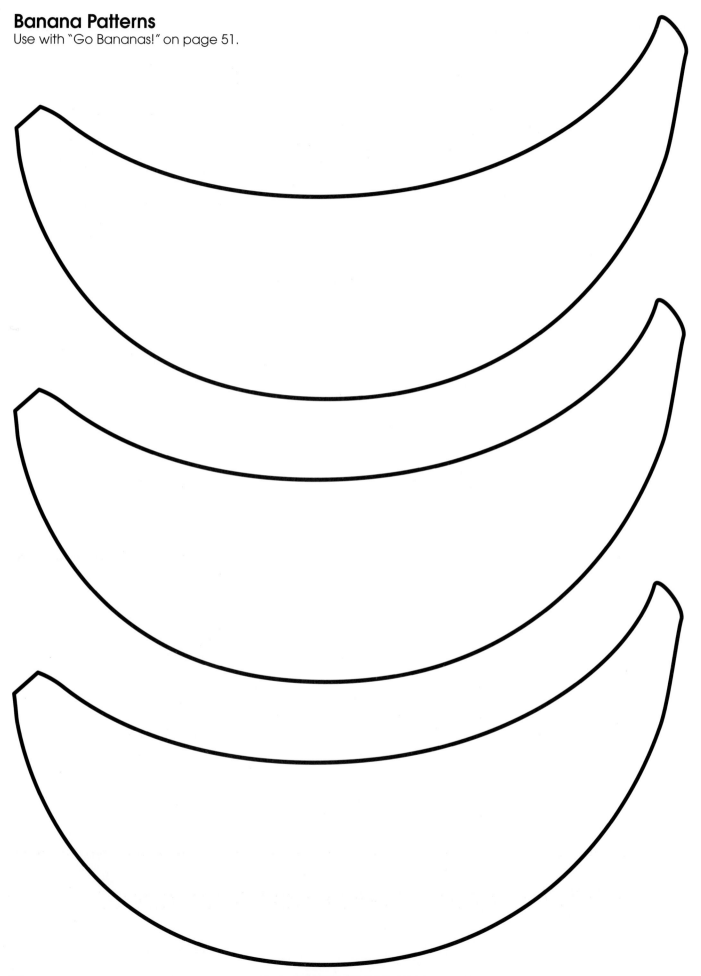

Name _____

Grapes and Raisins

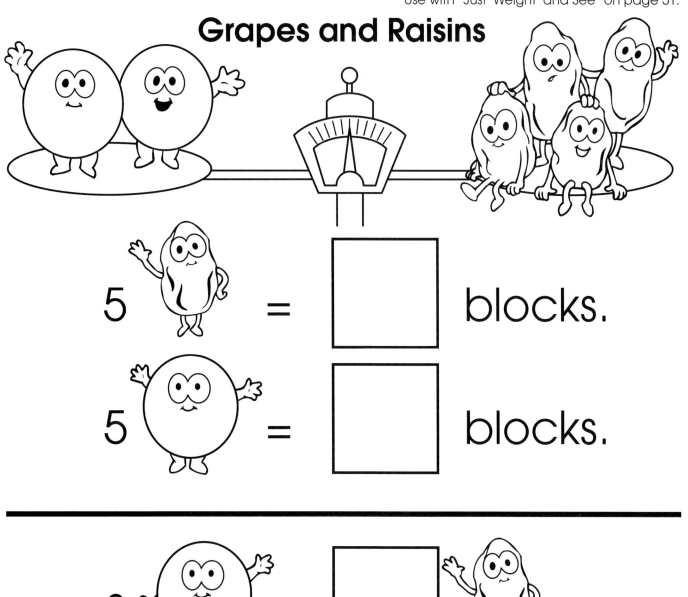

5 = ☐ blocks.

5 = ☐ blocks.

3 = ☐

10 = ☐

Think: Why do grapes weigh more than raisins?

Wonders Never Cease

Simple Science for Young Children

Making Changes

Have you heard it said that nobody likes change? Well, your classroom scientists will be the exception to that rule! Use the ideas in this unit, along with scientific-process skills, to explore change.

ideas by Suzanne Moore

Objective: Students will observe, record, and make predictions about changes.

Vocabulary: cause

Read All About It

To introduce the topic of *changes,* share your choice of the books listed below. Ask children what changed in the book(s). Then encourage students to brainstorm a list of other changes they notice in their everyday lives. Write their ideas on chart paper. For added fun, write each item mentioned with a Change-ables marker (made by Crayola). Then offer the color changer marker to a child and ask him to trace over the original work. What happens? Change!

Changes, Changes
By Pat Hutchins

*From Cow to Ice Cream**
By Bertram T. Knight

Strega Nona's Magic Lessons
By Tomie dePaola

*Also in the Changes series: *From Wax to Crayon, From Wheat to Pasta,* and *From Metal to Music.*

Changes in Our Lives

- weather
- the sky
- clouds
- our ages
- the clock
- ice
- the trees
- water— gets hot and cold
- puppies
- the grass
- a cake if you bake it

The Building Blocks of Change

Provide a supply of blocks in front of your class. Select a small group of children to join you in the front. Have the remainder of the class close their eyes and begin counting aloud to 30. As the class counts, ask the children in the small group to work together to change the blocks in whatever way they'd like. When the class reaches 30, have the other children open their eyes and observe the blocks. Then ask the questions below. Repeat the process until every child has had a chance to be the *cause* of change.

Three Questions
1. Do you see a difference?
2. What changed?
3. What caused the change?

Pam Crane

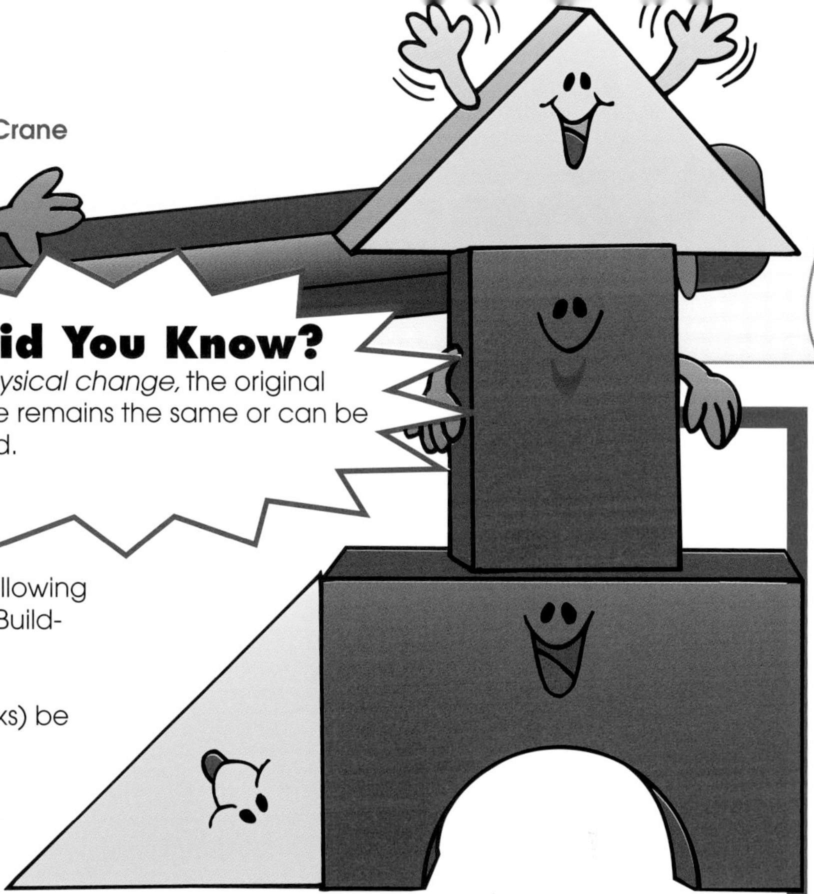

Did You Know?

In a *physical change,* the original substance remains the same or can be recovered.

Think About It

Prompt your youngsters to discuss the following questions in relation to the activity in "The Building Blocks of Change" on page 54.

1. Can the original substance (the blocks) be recovered?
2. What kind of change took place?

Change Back!

Try this simple activity to illustrate another type of physical change. Give each child a paper cup half-filled with clean sand. Instruct each child to add a little water to his cup and use a spoon to gently mix it up. Ask and discuss the three questions from page 54. Then ask children if and how the original substance can be recovered (changed back). Encourage children to record their predictions and then try out their ideas (such as letting the mixture sit out overnight or spreading it out on a paper towel). What happens? Do they think this change was a *physical change?* Why?

Foam on the Roam

You'll have everyone's attention with this small-group idea designed for scientific observation and loads of learning fun. In advance, cover a table with newspaper. Pour about a cup of vinegar into a bowl. Then give each child in the small group a clear plastic cup. Have each child scoop a tablespoon of baking soda into her cup. Ask each child what she thinks will happen if she adds vinegar to the baking soda. Then invite her to add one tablespoon of vinegar at a time to her cup. What happens? Ask and discuss the questions from page 54. Then ask the questions from "Think About It" on this page.

Did You Know?

When two or more substances mix together and form a new substance, this is called a *chemical change.* You can't easily get the original substance back again.

55

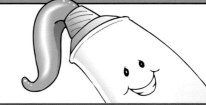

Wonders Never Cease
Simple Science for Young Children
Totally Teeth

Take a big bite out of science with these activities that tackle the topic of teeth!

ideas by Randi Austin and Susan Bunyan

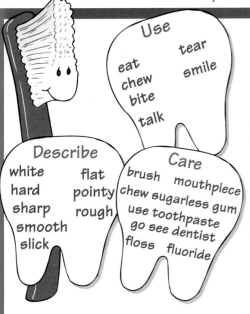

Use
eat   tear
chew   smile
bite
talk

Describe
white   flat
hard   pointy
sharp   rough
smooth
slick

Care
brush   mouthpiece
chew sugarless gum
use toothpaste
go see dentist
floss   fluoride

Observing
Classifying
Communicating

Dental Descriptions

Invite your little ones to sink their teeth into this descriptive activity. Prepare by making three large poster board cutouts of a tooth. Label one tooth "Describe," the second tooth "Use," and the last tooth "Care." You'll also want to collect enough handheld mirrors (ask parents to send some in) so that each child can have one.

Instruct each student to wash his hands thoroughly. Then give him a mirror and direct him to carefully observe his teeth. Starting with the first tooth cutout, ask students to name words or phrases that describe their teeth. List these responses on the tooth. Then continue with the second and third cutouts in this same manner. Display the three teeth nearby so that you can add any additional information that surfaces during the next activities.

Observing
Counting
Making a diagram

Tooth Types

Begin this activity by explaining to youngsters that they have three types of teeth. The front teeth are called *incisors;* they look thin and have straight, sharp edges. They are used for biting. The corner teeth are called *canines;* they have pointed edges and are used for tearing. The back teeth are called *molars;* they have bumpy surfaces and are used for chewing and grinding. Use the patterns on page 58 to show youngsters an enlarged copy of each tooth type. Then have each child use a mirror to locate each type of tooth in her own mouth.

Explain that a child's set of teeth contains four incisors, two canines, and four molars in both the upper and lower jaws. That's twenty teeth in all! Direct students back to their mirrors and challenge them to count their teeth. Then extend the learning by giving each student a copy of page 58. Have her use her own teeth as a reference as she cuts out the teeth types and then glues them to their respective positions. Save these toothy models for use in "Time for the Tooth Fairy!" on page 57.

Did You Know?
The enamel on your teeth (the white outer covering) is the hardest substance in your entire body.

Time for the Tooth Fairy!

Around the age of seven, most children begin to lose their baby teeth. The baby teeth's purpose is to hold the place for permanent teeth and help guide them into their correct positions. They are also important for the development of speech and chewing. By the age of 21, almost everyone has a complete set of permanent teeth—32 in all!

Have any of your students lost a tooth? If so, give each of them an opportunity to share her experience. Then have each child use the model made in "Tooth Types" on page 56 to record which tooth (or teeth) was lost by shading it in. Store the models in a notebook so that whenever that magical time of losing a tooth occurs, the lucky student can document it. Send the models home at the end of the year so that students can continue to keep track of their losses.

Predicting
Observing
Experimenting
Inferring relationships

Teeth-Friendly Foods

Sugar can be a harmful agent in tooth decay. It provides energy to plaque, helping it grow bigger and thicker. Some bacteria in plaque can even turn sugar into a sticky substance that helps the plaque stick better to a tooth's surface. Make this more concrete for your youngsters by doing this simple experiment.

Gather a carrot, an apple, a large marshmallow, a chewy chocolate bar, and four plastic knives. Explain the above information to youngsters. Have a child use a knife to cut one of the foods. Repeat this three times. Tell the students to imagine the knives are actually teeth biting into these foods. What happens? The foods containing more of the harmful sugars stick to the teeth (knives). If the teeth are not cleaned promptly, this could be the beginning of tooth decay.

Did You Know?

Toothbrushing is simply not enough. Toothbrushes can't reach the plaque that may be forming in between the teeth and below the gumlines. Failing to floss leaves about 35 percent of a tooth's surface uncleaned. People need to floss daily and make regular visits to the dentist for preventive treatments.

Name ______________________________

Totally Teeth!

Cut.
Glue.

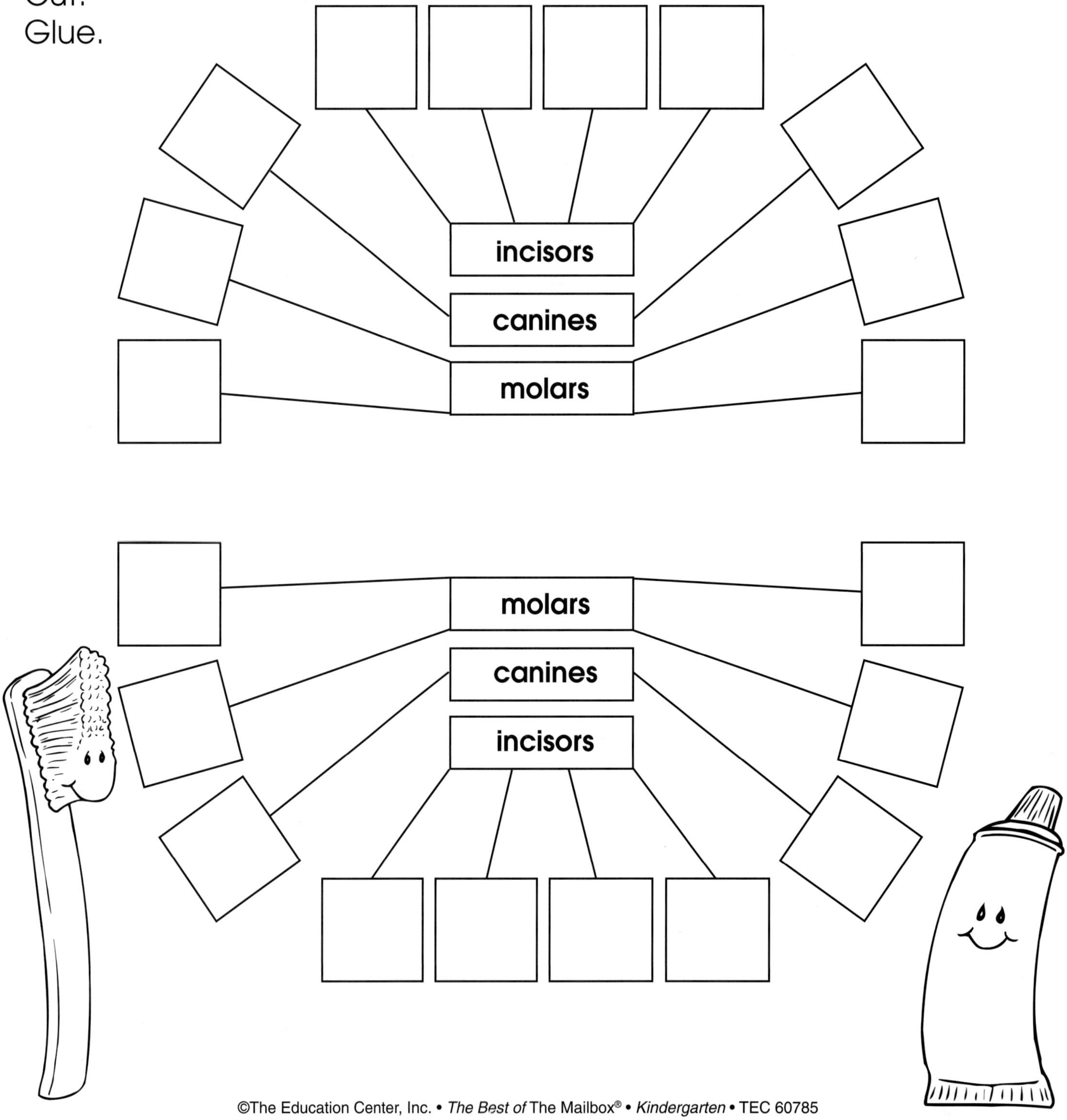
incisors
canines
molars
molars
canines
incisors

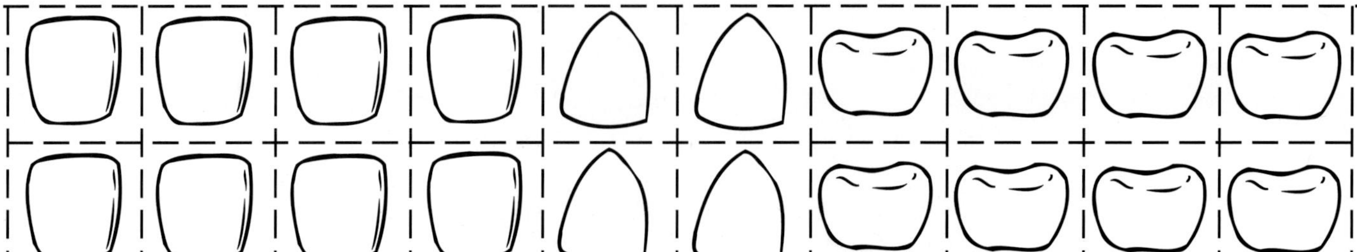

 Note to the teacher: Use with "Tooth Types" on page 56.

Wonders Never Cease
Simple Science for Young Children
Exploring Paper
Here's a pack of paper explorations hot off the press!

ideas contributed by Suzanne Moore

Objective: Students will explore the different properties of paper.

Getting Ready: To prepare for these studies, duplicate the parent note on page 62 for each child in your class. Several days before you begin this unit, send home a note with each child.

Dear Parent,
We are exploring all types of paper at school.
Please help your child find a paper product from
home and send it to school by _____ (date)
We will use these products in a class display. Thank
you for supporting your child's learning!

(teacher)

©The Education Center, Inc. • THE MAILBOX® • Kindergarten • April/May 2000

Paper, Paper Everywhere!

Begin your paper exploration with this circle-time activity and display idea. Gather youngsters together with the paper products they brought from home. Read *Paper, Paper Everywhere* by Gail Gibbons. Then have youngsters share their paper products with the class. Write the name of each product on a sheet of chart paper. Next mount a large paper tablecloth on a bulletin board. Then mount the chart on the tablecloth. Staple the students' paper products around the chart and then add a title. Display the board throughout your paper studies. As students discover other paper products, be sure to add them to the display. Paper *is* everywhere!

Paper, Paper!

cup
plate
hat
bag

Paper	Predictions	Observations and Findings
Waxed Paper		
Paper Towel		
Toilet Paper		
Construction Paper		
Index Card		

A Spoonful of Water

Will all types of paper soak up water? Set up this small-group activity and find out! In advance, gather a variety of types of paper—such as waxed paper, paper towels, toilet paper, construction paper, and index cards. Next, program a chart similar to the one shown; then glue corresponding paper samples in the appropriate boxes.

Invite a small group of students to examine the various types of paper and predict which ones will absorb water. Write their predictions on the chart. Next, have a child choose one type of paper. Place the paper on a tray and use an eyedropper to squeeze water onto the paper. Invite your students to carefully observe the paper and water. Did the paper absorb the water? Record students' findings and observations on the chart. When all of the paper samples have been tested, discuss youngsters' observations and findings.

Did You Know?
Most writing paper contains a water-resistant substance to prevent ink from spreading across the page.

Paper Blossoms

Writing papers resist water, but not all papers are water-resistant. Use this small-group activity to demonstrate how quickly some papers absorb water. To prepare, make a supply of construction paper flowers and cut them out. (See pattern on page 62.) Then make and cut out another supply of flowers on copier paper. Fold the petals of each flower as shown. Fill a plastic tub or bowl with water. Have youngsters examine the different flowers and predict what will happen when they are placed in the water. Then place a construction paper flower and a copier paper flower in the water as shown. The construction paper flower will open up quickly. The other flower will open slowly, if at all.

What happened? Most construction paper is not water-resistant. The paper absorbed the water, causing the petals to open. Copier paper is designed to resist water. Therefore, that flower opened slowly.

1.

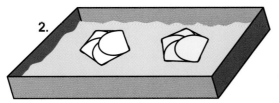

2.

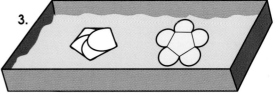

3.

Ahhh-choo!

Need a tissue? Facial tissues, toilet paper, and paper towels are some examples of highly absorbent paper. How do they absorb? Use this activity to uncover the secret ingredient! In advance, gather two small cups, a box of tissues, and a pencil. Fill one cup with water one-fourth inch below the rim. Then fill the second cup with tissues and count the number needed. Next have students predict how many tissues will fit inside the cup of water. Place one tissue in the cup and use the pencil to press the tissue to the bottom. Direct students to notice any air bubbles in the water. Continue adding tissues to the cup in this manner. When the cup is full, discuss the number of tissues needed to fill it. Students may be surprised to find that *more* tissues could fit inside the cup of water! How is that possible? Highly absorbent papers, like tissues, contain a lot of air. Pushing the tissue down in the water frees the air. Without air, there is a lot less tissue and more room in the cup! So what's the secret ingredient in highly absorbent paper? Air!

Paper Power!

Use this activity to demonstrate how to make a sheet of paper stronger. To prepare, gather a set of blocks, a small paper cup, a sheet of construction paper, and a supply of pennies. Use the blocks and paper to form a bridge. Then place the cup in the middle of the paper. Have students predict how many pennies the paper will hold. Invite your little ones to count as you place pennies in the cup one at a time. Continue until the paper falls under the weight. Compare students' predictions to the actual results.

Next, accordion-fold the same sheet of construction paper and place it back on the blocks as shown. Set the cup in the middle of the paper. Have students predict how many pennies the folded paper will hold and then repeat the experiment. The folded paper will hold more pennies! Why? The folds in the paper make it stiffer, allowing it to hold more weight. **Note:** Remove pennies from students' reach after the demonstration.

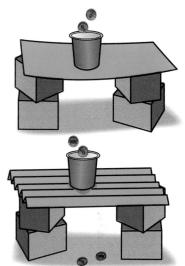

Did You Know?
The accordion folds in corrugated cardboard boxes are designed to increase the strength of the box.

Paper Matching

Stimulate youngsters' sense of touch with this unique matching game. To prepare, gather a variety of papers, such as corrugated cardboard, sandpaper, waxed paper, and paper towels. Next glue matching samples of paper onto pairs of index cards. Place the cards at a center along with a blindfold. To play, a child dons the blindfold and shuffles the cards. She then uses her sense of touch to find matching pairs. To check her work, the child removes the blindfold and looks at the cards.

I Saw the Light

Shed light on classification skills with this center! To prepare, stock the area with a few flashlights and a variety of paper, such as tissue paper, heavy cardboard, and construction paper in a variety of colors. Invite each child to visit the area and examine the papers. Have her predict which ones will allow light to shine through. Direct her to point a flashlight toward the ceiling, place a piece of paper over the light, and then turn it on. Can she see the light through the paper? Or does the paper block the light? Direct the child to sort the papers by their ability to block light. After all of the papers are sorted, invite the child to discuss her findings with you.

Parent Note
Use with "Getting Ready" on page 59.

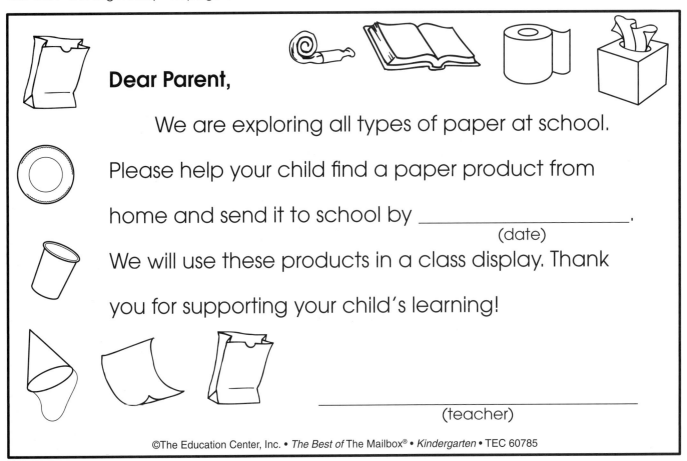

Dear Parent,

We are exploring all types of paper at school.

Please help your child find a paper product from

home and send it to school by _____.

(date)

We will use these products in a class display. Thank

you for supporting your child's learning!

_____
(teacher)

Flower Pattern
Use with "Paper Blossoms" on page 60.

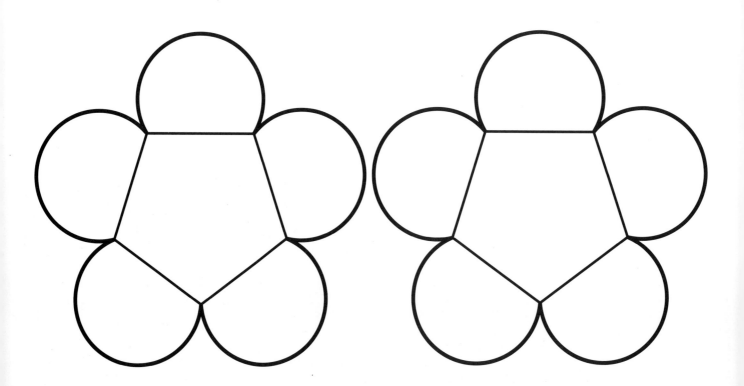

Mix Masters

Give youngsters a taste of what it's like to be a chemist with these easy and safe experiments focusing on mixtures and solutions.

ideas contributed by Suzanne Moore

Objectives:

1. Students will learn that a *mixture* is formed when two or more substances are combined and no reaction occurs.
2. Students will learn that a *solution* is a type of mixture.
3. Students will learn that mixtures can be separated.

Scientific Snack Mix

(makes 22 half-cup servings)

2 c. O-shaped cereal
2 c. Chex cereal
2¹/₂ c. raisins (15 oz. box)
2 c. M&M's candies

Scientific Snacking

Shake up student interest in mixtures with this idea that mingles a tasty learning experience with observation and communication skills. To prepare, make a class supply of the sorting sheet on page 66. Then gather the ingredients for "Scientific Snack Mix" (shown), one gallon-size resealable plastic bag, and one ¹/₂-cup measuring cup. During circle time, have students predict what will happen when all of the snack mix ingredients are combined.

To make the mix, pour all of the ingredients into the plastic bag and seal it. Pass the bag around the group and encourage each child to help mix the ingredients by gently shaking the bag. Next, use the measuring cup to serve each child a half cup of the mix on his sorting sheet. Explain that the snack is a *mixture,* a combination of two or more things that, when combined, can still be separated into its original parts. To demonstrate this concept, have the child sort his mixture by ingredients and then mix them back together to create the new snack. After sorting and mixing, invite little ones to munch on the scientific mixture. Mmm! Tasty!

Salt-and-Pepper Mix-Up

Get your little scientists set for more mixing fun with this small-group project. To prepare, fill a small bowl with salt and a small bowl with pepper. Have students examine the salt and pepper and then predict what will happen when they are shaken together. Next, provide each child with a snack-size resealable plastic bag; then have her place two spoonfuls each of salt and pepper into the bag. Help the child seal the bag; then direct her to vigorously shake the bag and mix the salt and pepper. Next, provide each child with a plastic magnifying glass and have her use it to examine the salt and pepper through the bag. Lead students to discover that bits of pepper can be seen through the salt. Guide your youngsters to conclude that the salt and pepper created a mixture. (If desired, save the salt-and-pepper mixtures to use in "Salt-and-Pepper Separation: The Sequel" on page 65.)

Did You Know?
When two materials mix thoroughly and evenly, a *homogeneous* mixture is created.

Sort and Snack

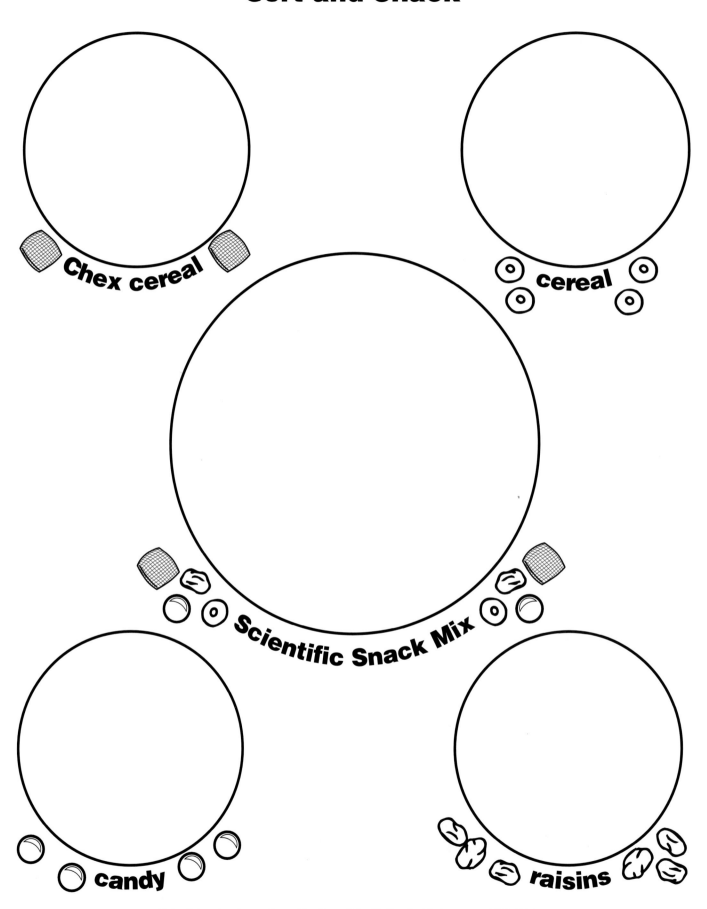

Chex cereal

cereal

Scientific Snack Mix

candy

raisins

©The Education Center, Inc. • *The Best of* The Mailbox® • *Kindergarten* • TEC 60785

Note to the teacher: Make a class supply of this sheet to use with "Scientific Snacking" on page 63.

Welcome to the Kindergarten Café

This special department of *The Mailbox®* magazine features recipes designed especially for the kindergarten child. Each cooking activity is seasoned with learning opportunities and generously sprinkled with fun. So read this introduction; then tie on your apron and get cooking!

What's in it For Me?

The cooking recipes in "Kindergarten Café" serve up meaningful practice in language arts, math, science, social skills, and more. When you incorporate these hands-on activities into your curriculum, your students will benefit in many ways. Here are just a few of them:

- Oral language and vocabulary development
- Emergent reading skills
- Counting practice and numeral recognition
- Sensory experiences
- Measurement exploration
- Following step-by-step directions
- Sequence
- Developing independence

Getting Ready

If this is your first experience with "Kindergarten Café," here are a few hints to ensure that each cooking experience will be deliciously successful:

- Create your cooking center in an area that has child-height work spaces and is near an electrical outlet. Decorate (or have children decorate) this area with cooking-related pictures, such as child-drawn or cutout pictures of homemade goodies. Mount the words "Kindergarten Café" near your cooking area.

- You also might like to host a yearly Grand Opening ceremony to equip your center and to stir up a batch of adult cooking volunteers. In advance, prepare an invitation indicating the cooking supplies needed in your cooking center. Have each child color an invitation and deliver it home to his parent. On opening day, display all the donated items. Serve snacks as you discuss the abundance of learning opportunities that a cooking center will provide for each parent's child.

Cooking Extensions

Extend the fun and learning of "Kindergarten Café" with the following ideas:

- Take a photo of each cooking experience. Insert the photo and a copy of the recipe in a photo album. Have students dictate about the cooking experience, and include their comments in the album.

- After each cooking experience, conduct a class survey. Label a graph as desired (such as "I loved it!", "It was okay," and "I didn't care for it"). Ask each child to write his name in the appropriate column. When the graph is complete, include it in the photo album.

- Cut out labels from products used in the cooking center. Insert these labels in the photo album, or glue the labels to a chart to add to your writing center.

- To help children with measuring and pouring skills, also provide a set of measuring spoons and measuring cups for your sand and/or water table.

Kindergarten Café

To prepare for each cooking activity, make a class supply plus one extra of the recipe cards (pages 70–71). Color one copy of the recipe cards; then cut the cards apart. Display the sequenced, colored cards in your cooking center. Arrange the ingredients and utensils near the recipe cards. As a small group of children visits the cooking center, ask each child to color a recipe and cut the cards apart. Have him sequence his cards and staple them together, creating a recipe booklet. After each cooking event, encourage the child to take his recipe home and keep it in a box to make a collection of his very own recipes.

Funny Fruit Face

Ingredients for one:
shredded cheese (hair)
canned pear half (head)
2 raisins (eyes)
maraschino cherry half (nose)

Utensils and supplies:
paper plate for each child
plastic fork for each child

Teacher preparation:
• Drain pears.
• Cut maraschino cherries in half.
• Arrange the ingredients, utensils, and supplies for easy student access.

Allison Pratt—Gr. K
Eagle Bluff Kindergarten
Onalaska, WI

School Bus Snack

Ingredients for one:
graham cracker (4 sections)
yellow-tinted vanilla frosting
4 pieces of Chex cereal
2 Mini Oreo cookies

Utensils and supplies:
paper plate for each child
plastic knife for each child

Teacher preparation:
• Tint vanilla frosting with yellow food coloring.
• Arrange the ingredients, utensils, and supplies for easy student access.

Melissa Hauck—Grs. PreK–1
Pear Tree Point School
Darien, CT

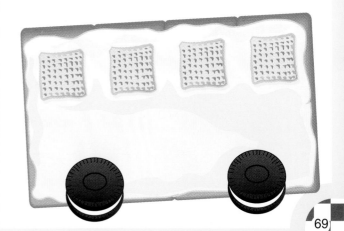

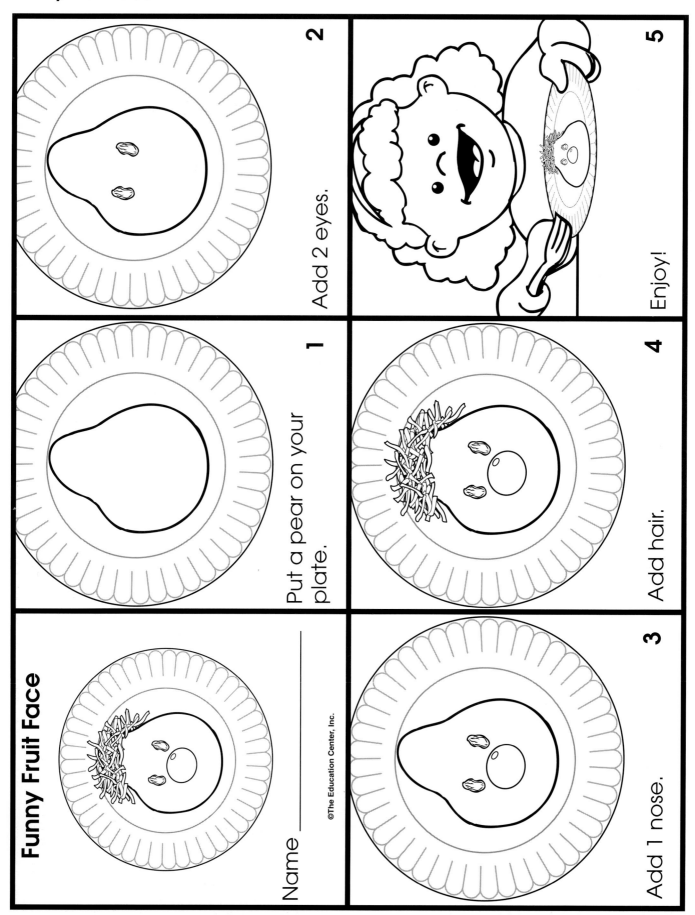

Funny Fruit Face

Name _____

©The Education Center, Inc.

1
Put a pear on your plate.

2
Add 2 eyes.

3
Add 1 nose.

4
Add hair.

5
Enjoy!

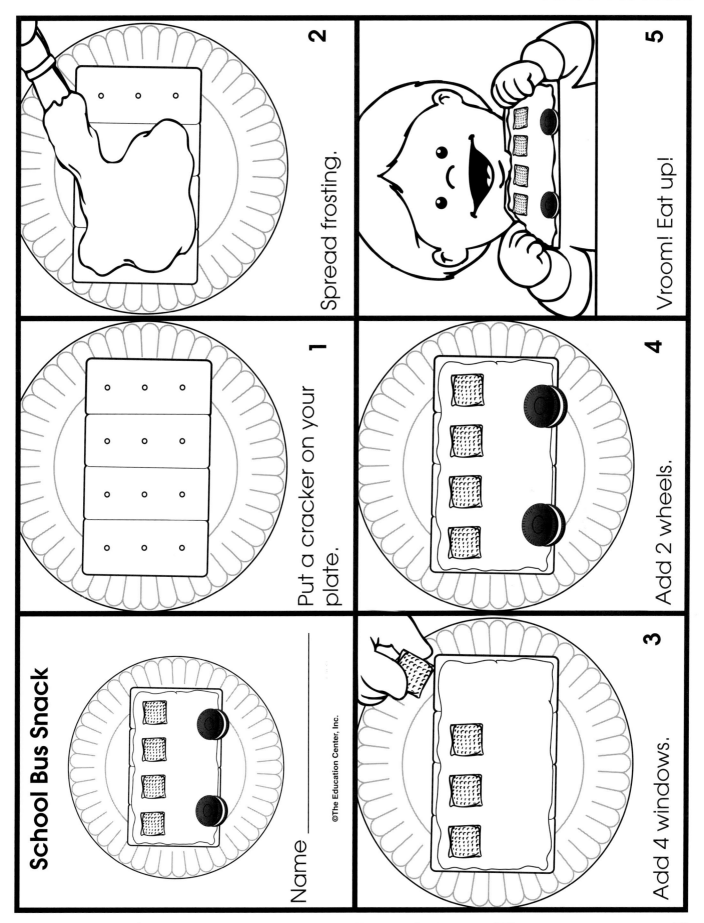

2

Spread frosting.

5

Vroom! Eat up!

1

Put a cracker on your plate.

4

Add 2 wheels.

School Bus Snack

Name _____

©The Education Center, Inc.

3

Add 4 windows.

Kindergarten Café

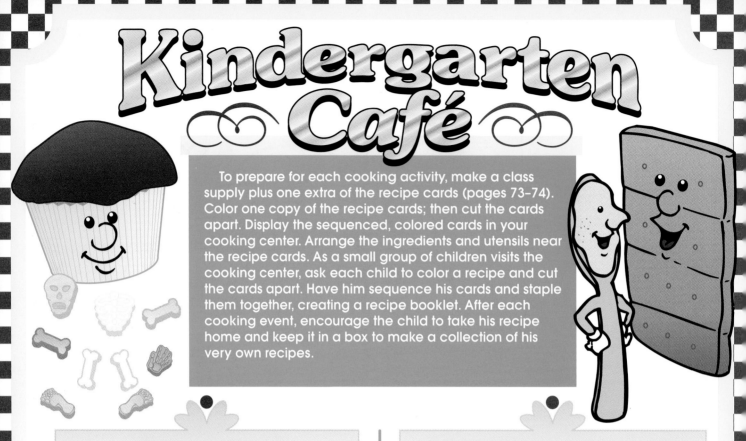

To prepare for each cooking activity, make a class supply plus one extra of the recipe cards (pages 73–74). Color one copy of the recipe cards; then cut the cards apart. Display the sequenced, colored cards in your cooking center. Arrange the ingredients and utensils near the recipe cards. As a small group of children visits the cooking center, ask each child to color a recipe and cut the cards apart. Have him sequence his cards and staple them together, creating a recipe booklet. After each cooking event, encourage the child to take his recipe home and keep it in a box to make a collection of his very own recipes.

Skeleton Snack

Ingredients for one:
cupcake
chocolate frosting
Brach's Dem Bones candy

Utensils and supplies:
paper plate for each child
plastic knife for each child

Teacher preparation:
- Bake cupcakes according to package directions.
- Arrange the ingredients, utensils, and supplies for easy student access.

adapted from an idea by Sue Lewis Lein—Gr. 4K
St. Pius X Grade School
Wauwatosa, WI

Upside-Down Pumpkin Pie

Ingredients for one:
$\frac{1}{3}$ c. vanilla pudding flavored with pumpkin pie spice
1 tsp. canned pumpkin
2 tsp. graham cracker crumbs

Utensils and supplies:
clear plastic cup for each child
plastic spoon for each child
$\frac{1}{3}$ c. measuring cup

Teacher preparation:
- Prepare pudding according to package directions.
- Mix in one-fourth teaspoon of pumpkin pie spice per box of pudding.
- Crush graham crackers.
- Arrange the ingredients, utensils, and supplies for easy student access.

Cynthia Jamnik—Gr. K, Our Lady Queen of Peace School
Milwaukee, WI

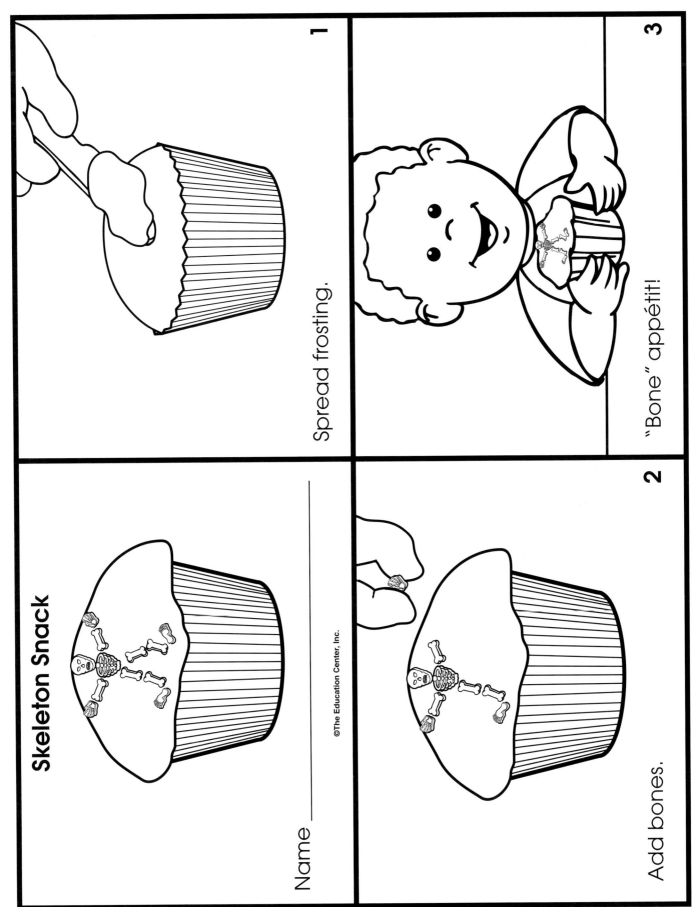

1

Spread frosting.

3

"Bone" appétit!

Skeleton Snack

Name _____

2

Add bones.

Recipe Cards
Upside-Down Pumpkin Pie

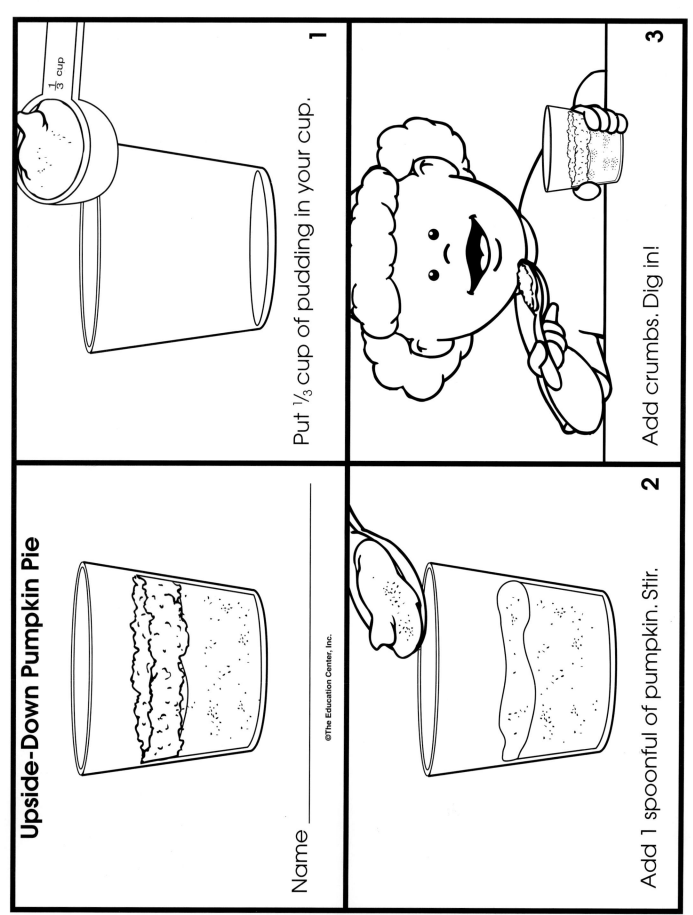

1

Put ⅓ cup of pudding in your cup.

3

Add crumbs. Dig in!

Upside-Down Pumpkin Pie

Name _____

©The Education Center, Inc.

2

Add 1 spoonful of pumpkin. Stir.

Kindergarten Café

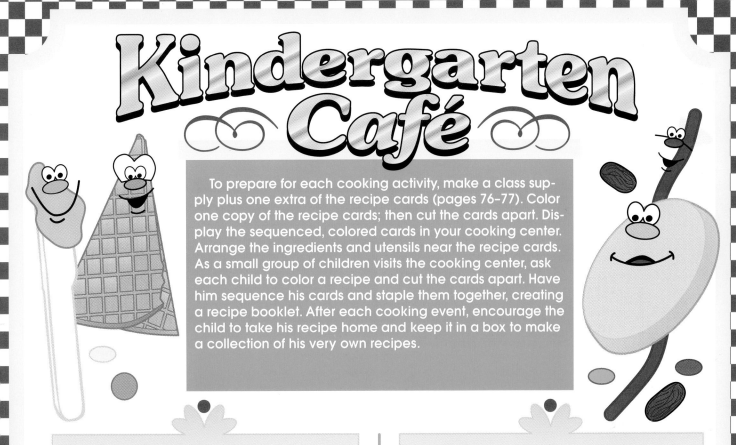

To prepare for each cooking activity, make a class supply plus one extra of the recipe cards (pages 76–77). Color one copy of the recipe cards; then cut the cards apart. Display the sequenced, colored cards in your cooking center. Arrange the ingredients and utensils near the recipe cards. As a small group of children visits the cooking center, ask each child to color a recipe and cut the cards apart. Have him sequence his cards and staple them together, creating a recipe booklet. After each cooking event, encourage the child to take his recipe home and keep it in a box to make a collection of his very own recipes.

A Tasty Tree

Ingredients for one:
pointed sugar cone
vanilla frosting tinted green
M&M's Minis candy pieces (ornaments)
yellow sugar crystals

Utensils and supplies:
paper plate for each child
plastic knife for each child

Teacher preparation:
- Tint the frosting with green food coloring.
- Arrange the ingredients, utensils, and supplies for easy student access.

Merry Mouse Cookie

Ingredients for one:
sugar cookie
vanilla frosting
2 raisins (ears)
3 M&M's Minis candy pieces (eyes and nose)
3" length of red licorice lace (tail)

Utensils and supplies:
paper plate for each child
plastic knife for each child

Teacher preparation:
- Cut licorice laces into three-inch lengths.
- Arrange the ingredients, utensils, and supplies for easy student access.

Recipe Cards
A Tasty Tree

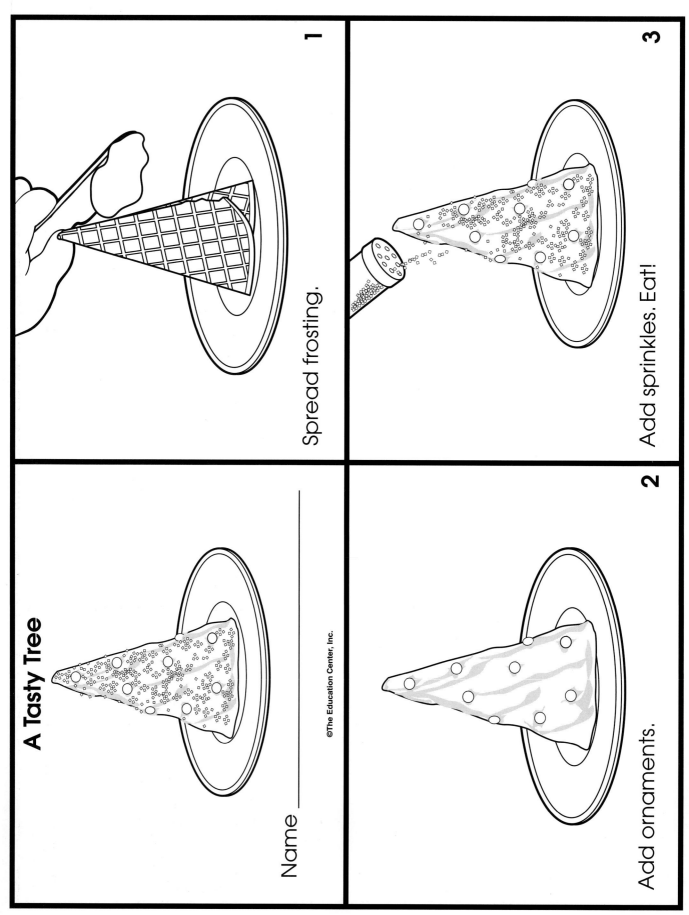

1

Spread frosting.

3

Add sprinkles. Eat!

A Tasty Tree

Name _____

©The Education Center, Inc.

2

Add ornaments.

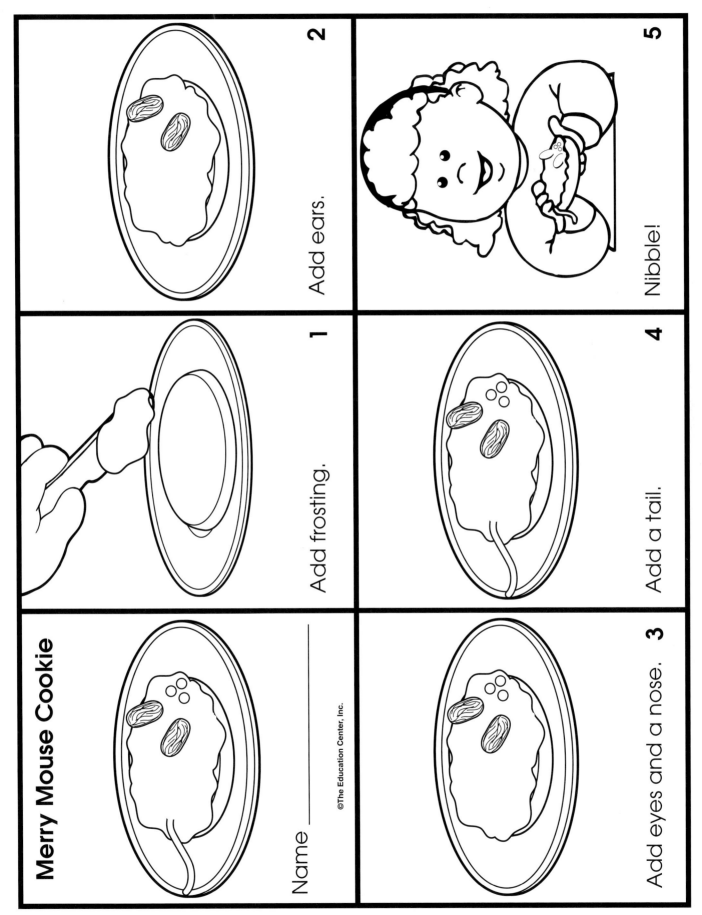

2

Add ears.

5

Nibble!

1

Add frosting.

4

Add a tail.

Merry Mouse Cookie

Name _____

©The Education Center, Inc.

3

Add eyes and a nose.

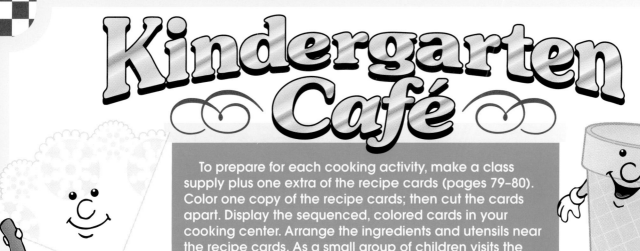

Kindergarten Café

To prepare for each cooking activity, make a class supply plus one extra of the recipe cards (pages 79–80). Color one copy of the recipe cards; then cut the cards apart. Display the sequenced, colored cards in your cooking center. Arrange the ingredients and utensils near the recipe cards. As a small group of children visits the cooking center, ask each child to color a recipe and cut the cards apart. Have him sequence his cards and staple them together, creating a recipe booklet. After each cooking event, encourage the child to take his recipe home and keep it in a box to make a collection of his very own recipes.

Lovebug Cookie

Ingredients for one:
large sugar cookie
strawberry-flavored frosting
2 pretzel sticks (antennae)
2 red M&M's candies (antennae)
2" piece of red licorice lace (mouth)
2 M&M's candies (eyes)
mini chocolate chip (nose)

Utensils and supplies:
paper plate for each child
plastic knife for each child
2 doily quarters (wings)

Teacher preparation:
- Cut licorice into two-inch lengths.
- Cut white doilies into quarters.
- Arrange the ingredients, utensils, and supplies for easy student access.

Peggy Stratton
Okeechobee, FL

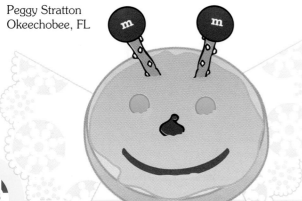

Cat in the Hat Snack

Ingredients for one:
scoop of vanilla ice cream
mini ice-cream cone wrapped with a strip of red Fruit by the Foot snack
3 M&M's candies
six 1" pieces of black or red licorice lace

Utensils and supplies:
paper plate for each child
plastic spoon for each child

Teacher preparation:
- Use an ice-cream scoop to scoop balls of ice cream onto a cookie sheet and then place the sheet in the freezer.
- Cut licorice into one-inch lengths.
- Cut red Fruit by the Foot snack into four-inch strips. Wrap one strip around each cone.
- Arrange the ingredients, utensils, and supplies for easy student access.

Terry Schreiber—Gr. K
Holy Family School
Norwood, NJ

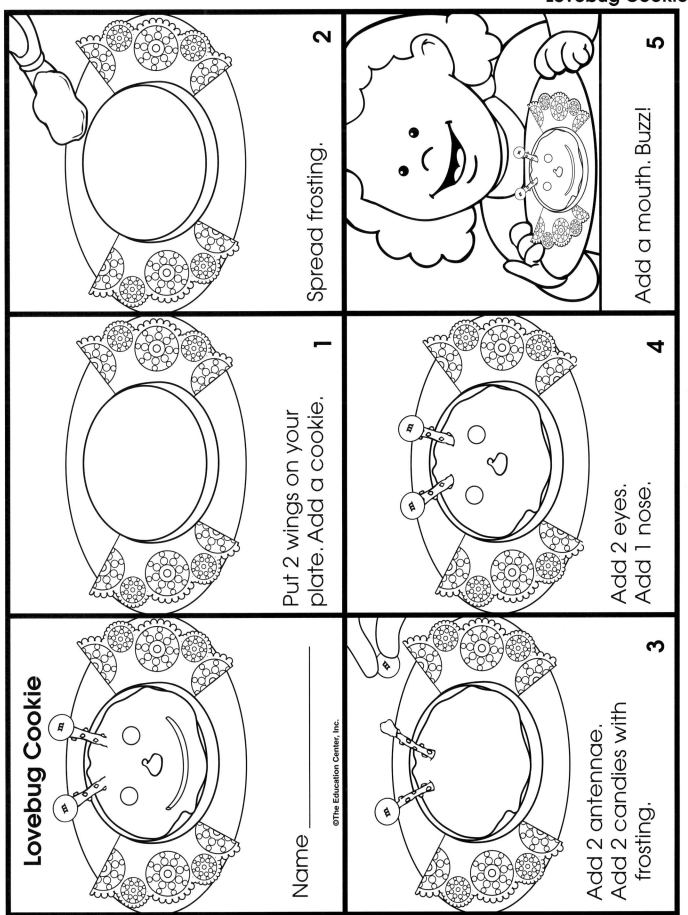

2

Spread frosting.

5

Add a mouth. Buzz!

1

Put 2 wings on your plate. Add a cookie.

©The Education Center, Inc.

4

Add 2 eyes.
Add 1 nose.

Lovebug Cookie

Name _____

3

Add 2 antennae.
Add 2 candies with frosting.

Recipe Cards
Cat in the Hat Snack

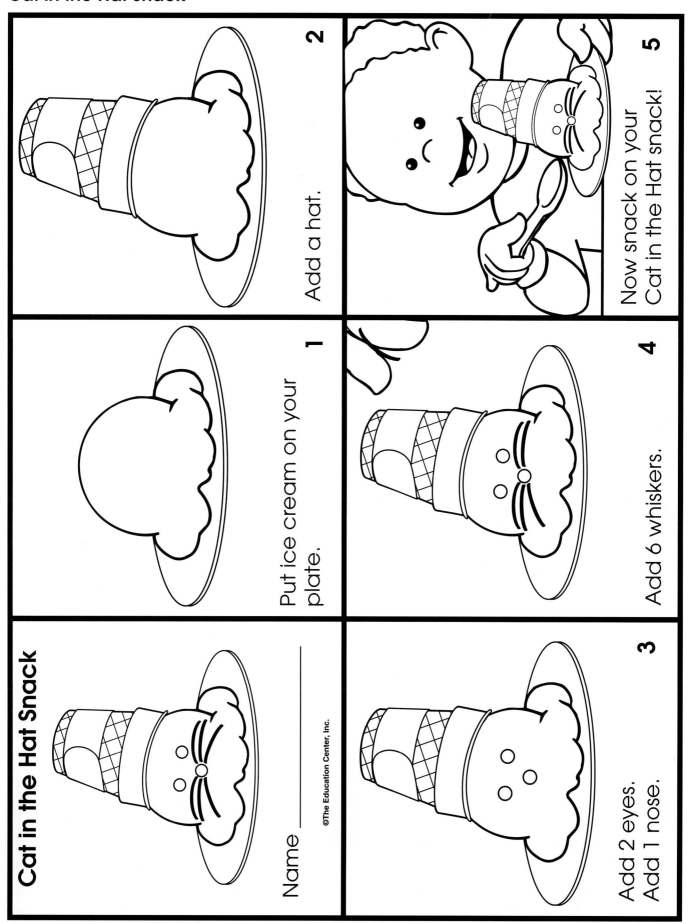

2

Add a hat.

5

Now snack on your
Cat in the Hat snack!

1

Put ice cream on your
plate.

4

Add 6 whiskers.

Cat in the Hat Snack

Name _____

©The Education Center, Inc.

3

Add 2 eyes.
Add 1 nose.

Kindergarten Café

To prepare for each cooking activity, make a class supply plus one extra of the recipe cards (pages 82–83). Color one copy of the recipe cards; then cut the cards apart. Display the sequenced, colored cards in your cooking center. Arrange the ingredients and utensils near the recipe cards. As a small group of children visits the cooking center, ask each child to color a recipe and cut the cards apart. Have him sequence his cards and staple them together, creating a recipe booklet. After each cooking event, encourage the child to take his recipe home and keep it in a box to make a collection of his very own recipes.

Bird's Nest

Ingredients for one:
3" square of Rice Krispies Treats
3 chocolate eggs
marshmallow chick

Utensils and supplies:
paper plate for each child

Teacher preparation:
- Prepare Rice Krispies Treats according to package directions.
- Arrange the ingredients, utensils, and supplies for easy student access.

adapted from an idea by Kathy Peake—Gr. K
A. W. Holloway School
Mobile, AL

Tasty Traffic Light

Ingredients for one:
graham cracker section
chocolate frosting
3 M&M's candies (one each of red, yellow, and green)

Utensils and supplies:
paper plate for each child
plastic knife for each child

Teacher preparation:
- Arrange the ingredients, utensils, and supplies for easy student access.

Rhonda L. Chiles—Gr. K
South Park Elementary
Shawnee Mission, KS

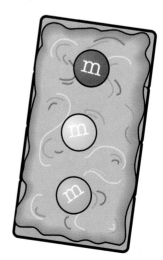

Recipe Cards
Bird's Nest

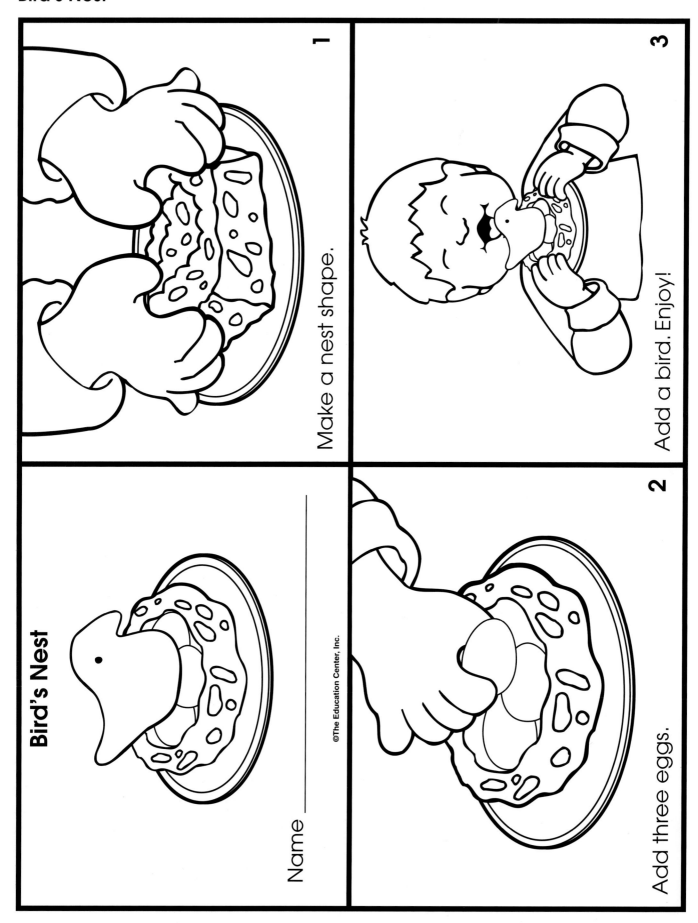

1 Make a nest shape.

3 Add a bird. Enjoy!

Bird's Nest

Name _____

©The Education Center, Inc.

2 Add three eggs.

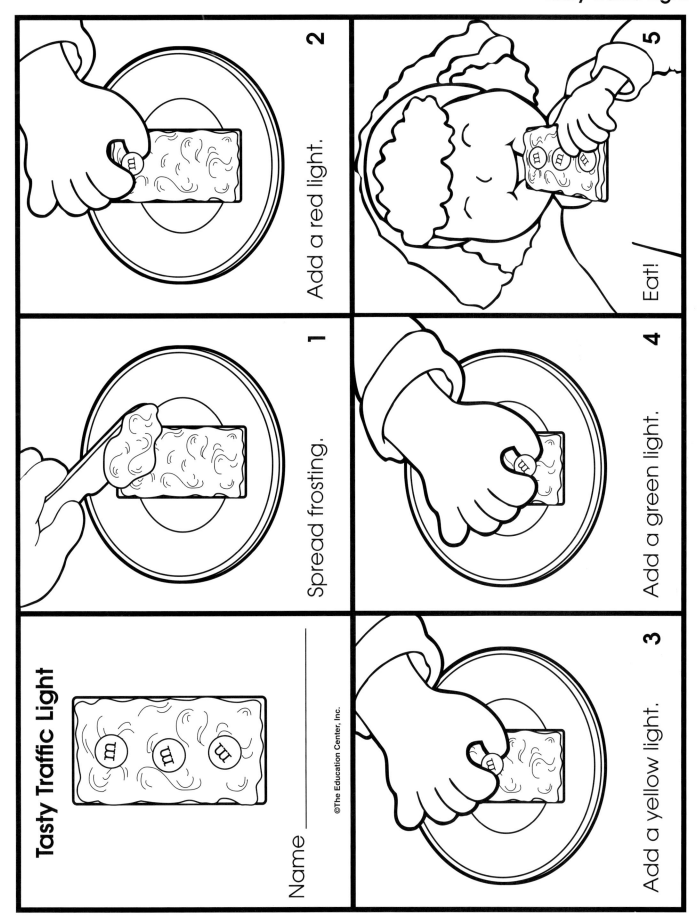

2

Add a red light.

5

Eat!

1

Spread frosting.

4

Add a green light.

Tasty Traffic Light

Name _____

©The Education Center, Inc.

3

Add a yellow light.

Kindergarten Café

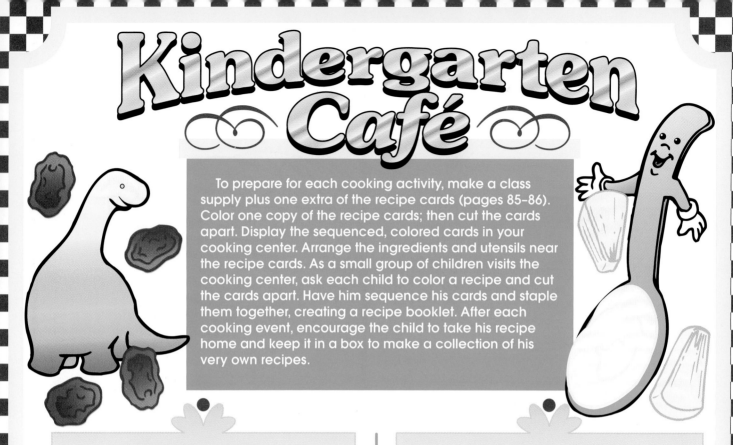

To prepare for each cooking activity, make a class supply plus one extra of the recipe cards (pages 85–86). Color one copy of the recipe cards; then cut the cards apart. Display the sequenced, colored cards in your cooking center. Arrange the ingredients and utensils near the recipe cards. As a small group of children visits the cooking center, ask each child to color a recipe and cut the cards apart. Have him sequence his cards and staple them together, creating a recipe booklet. After each cooking event, encourage the child to take his recipe home and keep it in a box to make a collection of his very own recipes.

Dinosaur Dig

Ingredients for one:
gummy dinosaur
½ c. Cocoa Pebbles cereal

Utensils and supplies:
small clear plastic cup for each child
plastic spoon for each child

Teacher preparation:
• Arrange the ingredients, utensils, and supplies for easy student access.

Rhonda Dominguez—Gr. 1
Rockbridge Elementary
Snellville, GA

Sunshine Salad

Ingredients for one:
spoonful lemon-flavored whipped topping
8 pineapple tidbits

Utensils and supplies:
paper plate for each child
plastic spoon for each child

Teacher preparation:
• Mix one large container of whipped topping with one large box of lemon-flavored gelatin powder and eight to ten drops of yellow food coloring.
• Arrange the ingredients, utensils, and supplies for easy student access.

adapted from an idea by Samantha Towne
Cordova, TN

1

Put a dinosaur in your cup.

3

Eat to excavate your dinosaur!

Dinosaur Dig

Name _____

©The Education Center, Inc.

2

Add rocks.

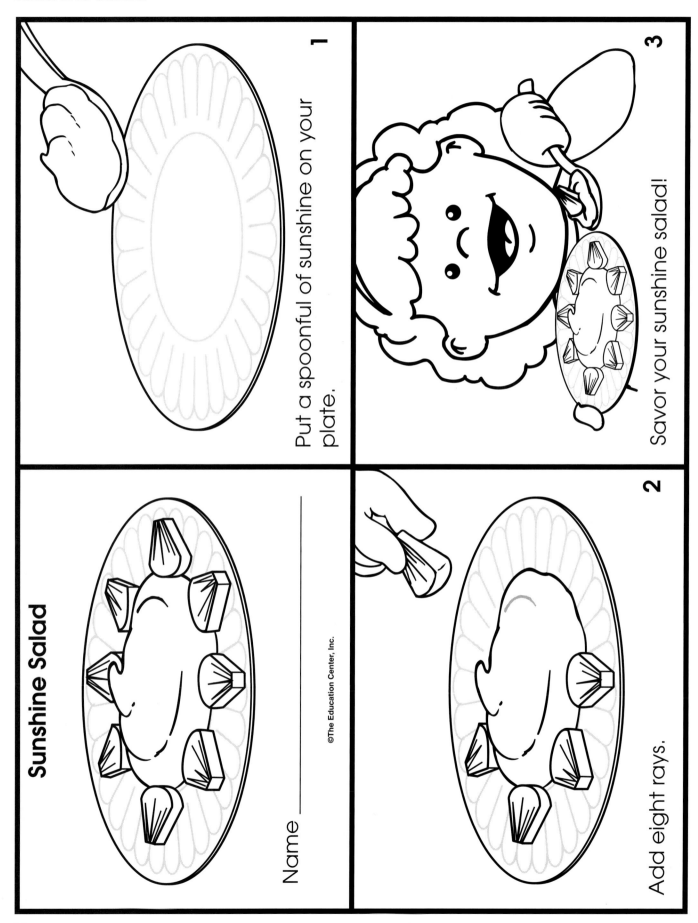

Sunshine Salad

Name _____

1
Put a spoonful of sunshine on your plate.

2
Add eight rays.

3
Savor your sunshine salad!

Rhythm & Rhyme Time

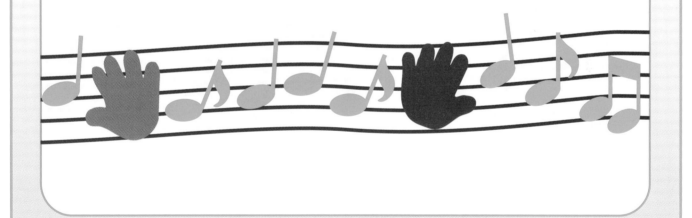

Rhythm & Rhyme Time

Calendar Song

Help youngsters understand the concepts of *yesterday, today,* and *tomorrow* by singing this song each day during your calendar time. Use a pointer to point to each day as you sing. Substitute the appropriate days of the week in each line and any appropriate information in the last line. You might mention a child's upcoming birthday, a special event at school, or a reminder that something is due.

(sung to the tune of "Mary Had a Little Lamb")

Yesterday was [Tuesday],
[Tuesday], [Tuesday].
Yesterday was [Tuesday].
Today is [Wednesday].

Tomorrow will be [Thursday],
[Thursday], [Thursday].
Tomorrow will be
    [Thursday],
And [we will go to art].

Sherry Galloway—Gr. K
WaKeeney Grade School
WaKeeney, KS

Pick a Pumpkin

It's pumpkin-pickin' time! Get your youngsters in the mood by singing this little ditty!

(sung to the tune of "London Bridge")

Pick a pumpkin from the vine,
Pumpkin round, pumpkin fine.
Pick a pumpkin from the vine.
Let's pick pumpkins!

Pick a pumpkin from the vine.
You pick yours; I'll pick mine.
Pick a pumpkin from the vine.
Let's pick pumpkins!

Betty Silkunas—Gr. K
Lower Gwynedd Elementary
Ambler, PA

Watch Out!

It's that time of year—ghosts and ghouls are lurking and searching for that big scare. Teach your little goblins this song and the accompanying motions. It's sure to turn those "ghasps" into "ghrins"!

(sung to the tune of "Santa Claus Is Coming to Town")

You'd better watch out! You'd better beware!
You'd better believe you're in for a scare!
Halloween is coming tonight!

Pumpkins aglow with snaggletoothed grins.
Skeletons jump right out of their skins.
Halloween is coming tonight!

Spooky, cackling witches are stirring up their brew.
Mean-faced, green-faced Frankensteins are coming after you!
BOO!

Repeat first stanza to end the song.

Diane ZuHone Shore—Gr. K
Marietta, GA

Point and shake finger.
Shiver.
Look wide-eyed.

Point to teeth.
Jump with arms out.
Look wide-eyed.

Stir with fists.
Walk stiff-legged.
Throw up hands.

Holiday Senses

Use this cute poem to revisit the five senses and then extend the poem into a brainstorming activity. Write each of the five senses on a separate sheet of chart paper. Then list holiday-related activities children name under the correct sensory headings. It's beginning to look, feel, taste, smell, and sound like Christmas!

At holiday time, it's nice to *see*
A lovely decorated Christmas tree.

At holiday time, it's nice to hear
Jingle bells ring on flying reindeer.

At holiday time, it's nice to feel
Santa's beard. Is it real?

At holiday time, it's nice to lick
A red-and-white striped candy stick.

At holiday time, it's fun to smell
Gingerbread cookies with sweet frosting gel.

Isn't it great? Isn't it fine
To use the five senses at holiday time?

Theresa Moonitz—Gr. K
Dr. Ronald McNair School P.S. 147 Q
Cambria Heights, NY

Hear
paper ripping—Rebecca
carols—Charles
"Ho! Ho! Ho!"—Mickayla
cash registers—Cassie
pots and pans—Trey
mixer—Blake
singing—Georgie

Goodbye

Settle your little ones and help them prepare for afternoon goodbyes with this simple poem. Each day substitute the next day of the week in the last line of the poem. Then encourage youngsters to hug one another before heading out the door!

It's goodbye time, don't you know?
The time of day for us to go.
We worked; we played; we had our fun.
Now let's hug goodbye
'Til [Tuesday] comes!

Meri Visnic—Gr. K
Manzanita School
Kingman, AZ

Crazy About Colors

Little ones will quickly learn to recognize colors with this song and activity. Provide each child with a set of crayons. After singing the last line of the song below, have students hold up the appropriate crayons and pretend to color.

(sung to the tune of "Paw Paw Patch")

Where, oh, where is dear little [red]?
Where, oh, where is dear little [red]?
Where, oh, where is dear little [red]?
Coloring the [apples] on the [apple tree].

Repeat, substituting the underlined words with other colors and phrases similar to the following: *yellow/lemons/lemon tree, orange/oranges/ orange tree, blue/berries/berry bush.*

Louise Duval—Gr. K, St. Joseph School, Webster, MA

89

A Penguin's Wish

This tune will help your little ones remember that penguins can't fly. Teach them the accompanying motions and have a waddling good time!

(sung to the tune of "I'm a Little Teapot")

I'm a little penguin, black and white.
I'm good at swimming, but not at flight.
When I'm in the ocean, I dive for fish.
Swimming's fun, but flying's my wish!

Point to yourself.
Make swimming motions; then shake head to say no.
Make diving motion with one hand.
Hook thumbs and wiggle fingers like wings.

Jean Zeller—Grs. K–4, WCSS St. William Campus, Waukesha, WI

Telephone Number Song

Memorizing a telephone number is a cinch with this quick little ditty! Simply substitute each youngster's telephone number and name in the verse below; then sing, sing, r-r-ring!

(sung to the tune of "London Bridge")

[123-4567], ring, ring, ring, ring, ring, ring.
[123-4567] is [Kent's] telephone number!

LeeAnn Stroud—Gr. K
Fountain Lake Elementary
Hot Springs, AR

Vowels!

Remembering vowels is easy when students learn with this simple song.

(sung to the tune of "Bingo")

There was a classroom full of kids
Who knew the vowel letters.
A, E, I, O, U
A, E, I, O, U
A, E, I, O, U
And sometimes letter Y too!

adapted from an idea by
Kristi Arndt—Gr. K
Lincoln HI Elementary
Hendricks, MN

A Planting Plan

Get all hands moving with this little ditty that reinforces the whole planting procedure.

(sung to the tune of "The Hokey-Pokey")

You scoop the soil in.
You pick the rocks out.
You poke the seed in,
And you pat it all about.
You add a little water
And you wait for it to sprout.
That's what it's all about!

Debra Kujawski—Gr. K, Southold UFSO, Southold, NY

Where Are the Bees?

This simple adaptation of the traditional chant will keep youngsters giggling! Have each child cut a beehive shape from construction paper; then help her glue the top of her beehive to another sheet of paper. When the glue is dry, gently lift and fold back the beehive. Provide ink pads and markers for the child to make five fingerprint bees that will be hidden under the hive. Then lower the hive back down on the paper. Teach your little ones the rhyme below and have them dramatize it using their hives.

Here is the beehive.
Where are the bees?
Hiding quietly where nobody sees.
Are you sure?
Let's peek in the hive.
One, two, three, four, five...OUCH!

adapted from an idea by Leslea Walker—Gr. K
Ridgeway Nursery School and Kindergarten
White Plains, NY

Our Friend, the Worm

Our gardens need worms! After discussing the benefits that worms provide, invite students to make these worm and flower props and then use them to dramatize the poem below. To make one flower, cut a flower shape from yellow construction paper. Then use a craft knife to cut a few slits through the center as shown. Turn the flower face-down. Apply glue around the rim of a foam cup and then press the cup down on the flower. Use a pencil to punch a hole in the bottom of the cup. To make a worm, wrap an adhesive bandage around the end of an unsharpened pencil. Then draw a face with a permanent marker. With a wiggle of the pencil, up pops a worm!

In My Garden
I was working in my garden.
I was clipping buttercups.
I was working in my garden,
When a worm just popped right up!

I looked at it and asked,
"What do you do?"
It looked back at me
And said, "I help you!"

Jane Wulf
Gainesville, FL

Leaving Kindergarten

Wrap up your end-of-the-year program by having students sing this catchy farewell song.

(sung to the tune of The Beverly Hillbillies *theme song)*

Come 'n' listen to our story 'bout what we did this year.
We've been workin' very hard, and we think that it's clear.
We've learned a lot of stuff and made some real good friends!
Now we're leavin' kindergarten but our learnin' doesn't end!

First grade! Bigger numbers, bigger words!

Nancy Shwartz
Consolidated School
New Fairfield, CT

I Love to Hike Outside

Encourage your youngsters to think of all the fun summer activities they love to participate in by teaching this little ditty. Substitute students' suggestions by replacing the underlined word in each line. Yippee, it's summertime!

(sung to the tune of "She'll Be Comin' Round the Mountain")

Oh, I love to [hike] outside in summertime.
Oh, I love to [hike] outside in summertime.
Oh, I love to [hike] outside,
Underneath the sky so wide.
Oh, I love to [hike] outside in summertime.

Suzanne Moore
Irving, TX

Alphabet Experts

Looking for a way to celebrate learning the alphabet? Invite your little ones to give themselves a pat on the back as they sing this catchy letter song.

(sung to the tune of "I've Been Working on the Railroad")

We've been working on our letters,
Learning the ABCs.
We've been working on our letters.
Just listen to us, please.

When you put letters together,
A word is what you'll get!
We will be terrific readers.
We know the alphabet!

Cindy Bowen—Grs. K–5
The Shepherd's Fold School
Hanover, PA

Lighting the Way to Literacy

Early Experiences in Reading & Writing

Lighting the Way

Early Experiences in Reading & Writing

B Sees D

Try this simple tip to help your youngsters remember *b* and *d* letter formations. Write *"b sees d"* on a 9" x 12" sheet of construction paper. Draw a face on each letter to show it looking at the other one; then post the sign in your classroom. Next, teach each child to make a lowercase *b* with her left hand and a lowercase *d* with her right hand. Have students recite the phrase *"b sees d"* as they look at their hands. When a child is confused about the direction *b* or *d* faces, just say *"b sees d"*!

Jessica Wells—Gr. K, Burlington, NJ

Eye Spy

Little ones will be keeping an eye on the alphabet when they follow your clues in this fun activity! For each child, create an eye-spy stick by hot-gluing a large wiggle eye to one end of a wooden craft stick. Give each child a stick and an individual alphabet chart. Supply clues for a particular letter and ask youngsters to look for that letter. Have students use eye-spy sticks to point to the letter. Clues might be "I am the fifth letter of the alphabet. I make the /e/ sound. I begin the word *elephant*." Hey—that's the letter *E!*

Rhonda L. Chiles—Gr. K, South Park Elementary, Shawnee Mission, KS

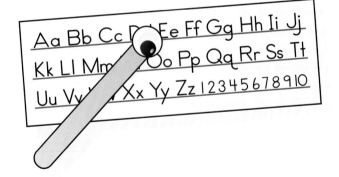

There's a "Friend-ergarten" in Kindergarten

This original rhyming book is sure to be a favorite in your classroom library. Read Dr. Seuss's *There's a Wocket in My Pocket!* Talk with students about the rhyming nonsense and real word pairs on each page. Have each child think of a place. Then instruct the child to name an imaginary creature by making a nonsense word that rhymes with his selected place. Next, give each child a 12" x 18" sheet of white construction paper and have him illustrate his creature. Then help each youngster complete a rhyming sentence for the illustration. Bind the completed pages and title the big book "There's a 'Friend-ergarten' in Kindergarten."

Jillian Rode—Gr. K, Shanghai American School, Shanghai, China

A gloor is on the door.

A splouse is on a house.

to Literacy

The Story Can

Just finished reading a story? Bring out the story can! Simply cover a clean, empty can with construction paper and the decorations of your choice. On each of several wooden craft sticks, print key words—such as *characters, setting, problem, solution, beginning,* and *ending*—to help youngsters discuss stories. Put the sticks in the story can. After reading a story aloud, show youngsters the can and explain the meanings of the words on the sticks. Then model how to draw one stick and talk about the element of the story indicated. Once students understand the concept, have volunteers draw sticks and discuss the story with the group. Use as many or as few sticks as you like after each story.

Karen Saner—Gr. K, Burns Elementary, Burns, KS

Take Note!

Next time you read a story or show your youngsters a video, pass out paper and pencils first! Ask your students to take notes (make simple drawings) about what they hear. Then have them recall important facts or interesting details with the help of their notes. This review method will really rev up reading comprehension!

John M. Barrera, Las Americas Early Childhood Development Center, Houston, TX

Jean Kowalski—Gr. K, Lincoln School, Alpena, MI

And

Youngsters will quickly learn the sight word *and* when you try this creative activity! Purchase a long length of wide pastel ribbon. Use a black permanent marker to write the word *and* on the ribbon two times, spacing the words as shown. Ask three students to stand and hold the ribbon in front of the group. Ask a child to make up a sentence about the three children, such as "John and Lin and Carly are in a row." Point to the students named and to the word *and* as the sentence is repeated by the whole group. Keep going with other students and new sentences until everyone has had a turn. For added fun, ask a fellow teacher or staff member to take a place behind the ribbon!

Judi Lesnansky—Title I, New Hope Academy
Youngstown, OH

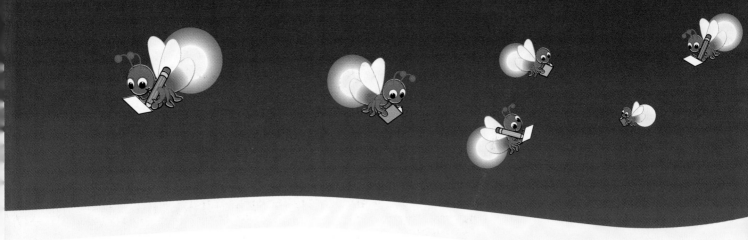

Good Point!

Use these pint-size pointers to motivate and point little ones toward literacy. To make one pointer, simply hot glue a seasonal pencil topper on the end of an unsharpened pencil. If needed, demonstrate how to use these nifty tools. Then set the pointers in your reading area and invite youngsters to use them as they read aloud. Point well made!

Mary Kulpa—Gr. K, St. Mary's School, Bloomington, IN

Tell About It!

Need a kindergarten-level book report idea? Try this pictorial version. Divide a sheet of chart paper into four sections and label each section as shown. Review the different parts of a story: *characters, setting, main events,* and *ending.* Then have each child (or small group of children) use a favorite book to complete a report. Instruct him to draw a picture for each section and then write or dictate to you information to describe his drawings. If desired, send the programmed chart, a book, and directions home to encourage parental involvement. After the charts are finished, invite each child to share his report. Communication skills really get a workout here!

Donna Peduto—Gr. K
Neshobe Elementary School
Brandon, VT

Word Sleeve

Slip some words into your word sleeve, and you'll be ready for youngsters to practice sounding out words! To make a word sleeve, decorate a sheet of construction paper and fold it into thirds; then staple the loose edges together. Cut a number of 2½" x 12" strips of tagboard. On each strip, write a word you'd like your students to sound out. To use the word sleeve, slip a word strip into it. Slowly pull the word out of the sleeve, revealing one letter at a time and challenging your kindergartners to sound it out. B-r-i-g-h-t idea!

Winnie Stine—Gr. K, Governor's Ranch Elementary, Littleton, CO

All
Together Now...

Games, Group Activities, and Circle-Time Ideas

All Together Now

Who's in the Spotlight?

Help your new kindergartners get acquainted with the help of this flashy activity! Have students stand in a circle. Invite one child to stand in the center of the circle and hold a flashlight. Instruct youngsters to say the chant below while the child in the center spins slowly, flashing the light on the students in the circle. At the end of the chant, have her stand still and name the child who is "in the spotlight." Then have the identified child take her place in the center of the circle and hold the light for the next round.

Round and round the flashlight twirls,
Shining on the boys and girls.
Will it stop on you or me?
One more spin, and we will see!
I see...

Karen Pasiuk
Old Saybrook, CT

Name Memory

With a little preparation, this game will entertain your students all year long! First, you'll need to gather a large supply of a material on which you can program letters, for example, ceramic tiles, milk caps, or tagboard squares. Use a permanent marker to write the letters of each child's name on separate pieces as shown. Put each set of letters in a Ziploc bag labeled with the matching name.

In small groups (or pairs), have students get their bags of letters and mix all the letters together. Then help them arrange the letters face-down in rows. To play, each child, in turn, turns over *one* letter. If that letter is used in his name, he keeps it. If not, it is turned back over. The first player to spell his name correctly (including an uppercase letter at the beginning) is the winner! This game can be more challenging as the year progresses by increasing the number of players. Now where was that *S*?

Michele Garza—Gr. K, Meridian Elementary, Meridian, TX

Circle Time That Counts

Here's a circle-time activity that's easy to build into your morning routine. Have each child bring a linking cube to morning group time. As you sing the song to the right, direct each child to link her cube to the others as they are passed around the circle and then pass the resulting stick to her neighbor. When all the cubes are attached, lead the class in counting the cubes aloud. If there are children absent, challenge youngsters to figure out which classmates are absent and determine how many cubes there will be when they return. Then finish the activity by singing the appropriate ending verse. Hooray!

Stacey Helders-Pevan—Gr. K
Prince of Peace, Milwaukee, WI

(sung to the tune of "London Bridge")

Add your cube and pass the stick, pass the stick,
     pass the stick.
Add your cube and pass the stick.
Watch it grow!

We will count them one by one, one by one,
     one by one.
We will count them one by one
When it's done.

Possible Last Verses:
Everyone is here today, here today, here today.
     (Or: All but [three] are here today...)
Everyone is here today.
Let's shout hooray.
HOORAY! *(spoken)*

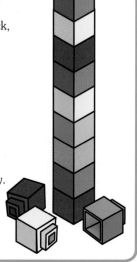

We Are Alike; We Are Different

Try this poster project to help emphasize to your little ones that all people are unique and special, but share many similarities too. In advance, take a head-and-shoulders photo of each child in your class. After discussing which characteristics people share and what things make each person unique, invite youngsters to look through magazines and cut out various pictures of people. Then label a sheet of poster board as shown. Have students take turns gluing the photos and picture cutouts onto the poster to make a collage.

Jennifer Weimann—Gr. K
Wollaston Child Care Center, Quincy, MA

We Are Alike;
We Are Different

The Caboose Is Loose!

Every child will want to be last in line when you play this fun outdoor game! Have children line up one behind another. Have the child in front walk, run, skip, or do whatever action she chooses as the others follow and imitate her. At some point, shout, "The caboose is loose!" At this time, the last child in line—the caboose—becomes It and begins to chase everyone else as they scatter and try to avoid being tagged. The child who is tagged becomes the caboose for the next round of play, and the former caboose becomes the leader. What fun!

Kimberly Bush—Gr. K, Oakland PreK and Gr. K, Oakland, NJ

The caboose
is loose!

Roll Over!

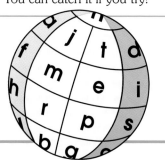

Use these cute manipulatives during a singing of "Ten in the Bed." Give each child an 8" x 5½" piece of tagboard, two cotton balls, nine craft sticks, and one wooden coffee stirrer. Help each child fold her paper, as shown, and staple the sides to make a pocket. Have the child use markers or stickers to decorate the pocket to resemble a bed. Then have her glue the cotton onto the pocket to make pillows. Next, instruct the child to use markers to draw a face on each of the sticks. Finally, have the child insert the sticks into her bed. Now she's ready for the sing-along. As each verse of "Ten in the Bed" is sung, have the child remove a stick person from her bed until only the little one is left. Good night!

Jennifer Barton—Gr. K, Elizabeth Green School, Newington, CT

Beach Ball Blast

Have some summer fun while reviewing the alphabet. Use a permanent marker to divide a beach ball into 26 sections. Write a different letter in each section. Teach your youngsters the chant at the right. Then arrange students in a circle. After reciting the chant, call out a child's name and toss the ball into the air. Encourage that child to catch the ball, look at the section that his right pointer finger is touching, and then name the letter (make the sound of the letter, name a word that begins with the letter, etc.). Have him toss the ball back to you, and begin the chant again. Continue until each child has had a turn. If desired, program another ball (with sight words or addition problems, for example) to review other skills. Ready? Catch!

adapted from an idea by Deb Scala—Gr. K, Mt. Tabor School, Mt. Tabor, NJ

Listen closely as I name
One of you to play this game.
I'll toss the ball up in the sky.
You can catch it if you try!

Circle-Time Jar

Help your students review concepts, skills, and songs they've learned throughout the year with the help of a simple jar! Each time you cover a new theme or skill with your class, jot down review questions or write down names of songs you've taught the class on individual slips of paper. Keep the slips of paper in your Circle-Time Jar, and continue to add to the jar throughout the school year. Each day at group time, pull out a slip (or two) and ask the question or announce the name of the song. Then invite students to answer or have everyone sing. Okay—who remembers the words to our Johnny Appleseed song?

Shannon Adams—Gr. K, Waxahachie Faith Family Academy
Waxahachie, TX

Name the five senses.

Mystery Reader

This name-oriented version of the traditional game Hangman helps students learn about vowels and consonants. To prepare, write "Mystery Reader" at the top of a board. Then make two columns labeled "Vowels" and "Consonants." Secretly choose a child to be the Mystery Reader, and write one blank for each letter in that student's name at the bottom of the board. Spelling that name is the purpose of the game!

To begin, have a student volunteer name a vowel and make its sound. Write the vowel in the "Vowels" column. Then students may ask if the letter is in the name of the Mystery Reader. If it is, write it in the proper blank. If not, cross it out. After listing and asking about all the vowels in the name, repeat the procedure with the consonants. When the Mystery Reader's name is revealed, have him help with choosing a book, reading a story, or using props during storytime.

Shannon Martin—Gr. K, Provena Fortin Villa, Bourbonnais, IL

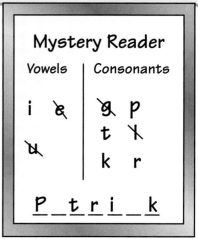

Raiding the Henhouse

Students will fine-tune their visual skills as they play this game. Show students six to eight different-colored plastic eggs and then place them in a basket. Select one child to be the fox and tell the others that they will be the hens. Have the hens cover their eyes while the fox removes an egg from the basket. Once the egg has been removed, the fox howls to signal the hens to uncover their eyes. In turn, have each hen guess which colored egg is missing. The child who guesses correctly becomes the next fox. For more challenge, have the fox remove more than one egg from the basket and have youngsters calculate the number of missing eggs.

Lori J. Brown—Pre-K
Lebanon Valley Brethren Home Day Care
Palmyra, PA

Happy Birthday, USA!

It's party time! Celebrate the birthday of the USA by making some patriotic party hats that look a bit like...well, birthday cakes! To make one, have a child paint wavy lines of white tempera paint "frosting" across a 6" x 24" strip of red construction paper or heavy red bulletin board paper. Then have him glue on a few stars cut from blue construction paper. Next, have him glue several construction paper candles (1" x 4" strips of blue and white construction paper) to the top of the strip. Then invite him to light the candles by gluing on small red paper flames. Wrap the strip around his head and staple the ends together for a perfect fit.

When everyone is dressed for the party, bring out a sheet cake decorated like the American flag and sing "Happy Birthday to You" to the good ol' USA!

Sue DeRiso—Gr. K, Barrington, RI

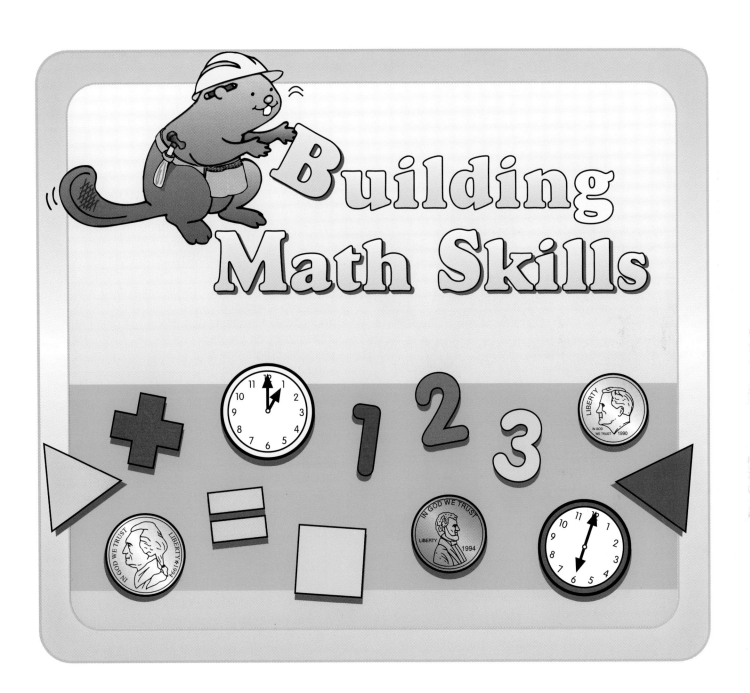

Building Math Skills

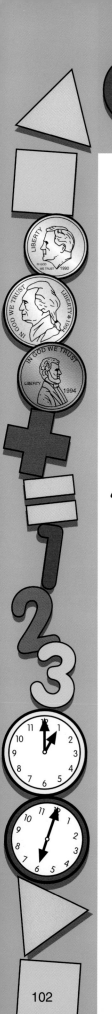

Building

One!

Two!

Three!

"Weight," There's More!

Youngsters' math skills will really measure up with this weighty idea. In advance, program a sheet of paper similar to the one shown; then make a construction paper copy for each child. To begin the activity, demonstrate the concept of heavy and light using a balance scale and a variety of objects, such as counting blocks, paper clips, or crayons. Next, have students brainstorm a list of things or people that are heavier than they are. Provide each child with a programmed sheet of paper, a construction paper strip, and a small triangle shape. Have her glue the strip and triangle on the paper as shown. Invite her to complete the programmed sentence. Write her response on her sheet of paper; then have her illustrate the sentence.

A _car_ is heavier than I am.

Cheryl Martin—Gr. K
Woodlake Elementary
San Antonio, TX

Counting

Sound Off!

Reinforce counting skills with this quick, easy-to-play game. Have your little ones stand in a circle. Call out a number that's appropriate for them to count to. Designate one child to start. He calls out "One!" and then the counting moves to the next child who says "Two!" and so on. The child who calls out the chosen number sits down. Then the counting begins again. Play continues until there is one child standing. Reward the efforts, call out another number, and start again! Who will be the lucky one this time?

Denise Saylor
Miller Heights Elementary
Bethlehem, PA

Identifying numbers
Counting

"Exer-dice"

Get kindergartners pumped up about learning higher numbers with this activity! Label each side of a cube-shaped gift box (stuffed with tissue) with any number from 11–19. Seat youngsters on the floor and toss the cube to a child. Have her identify the number that lands on top. Then have her choose an activity for the class to do, such as jumping jacks, clapping, or blinking. Have the number of repetitions match the number on the cube. Then instruct the child who chose the activity to toss the cube to someone else for another round.

Naomi Nussbaum, M.A.—Gr. K
Barnert Temple
Franklin Lakes, NJ

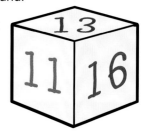

Math Skills

Guess the Missing Number

Chances are your youngsters will improve their number sequencing and name writing skills with this morning activity. Display a 100 number chart with removable number cards at students' eye level. Above the chart post a sign that reads "Guess the Missing Number and Win!" Place a supply of paper, pencils, and an empty container on a table nearby. Each morning remove one number card before students enter the classroom. Then invite each child to guess the missing number and write it on a slip of paper along with her first name. Then have the child drop it into the designated container. Reward stickers to students who have written their names and guessed the number correctly. As the year progresses, gradually remove larger numbers from the chart and require students to write their first and last names to qualify as winners.

Kimberly Wingard—Gr. K
Reynolds Elementary School
Greenville, PA

Counting Kernels

Fall is the perfect time to harvest number recognition and one-to-one correspondence. To prepare, cut out several ears of corn from yellow poster board. Then use a marker to divide each ear of corn into ten sections. Label each section with a different number from 1 to 10; then glue on green construction paper husks. Place the corn at a center along with a container of dried popcorn kernels. Invite each child to visit the center, choose an ear of corn, and then place the appropriate number of kernels in each section.

Vanessa King
Canterbury School
Atlanta, GA

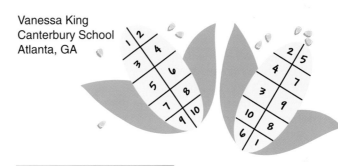

Class Math Journal

Your youngsters will look forward to math time with this personalized class journal. To make your class journal, add a supply of paper to a small three-ring binder. Every day write a story problem using one student's name. Have the featured child help solve the problem by drawing pictures to represent the story. As the year progresses, encourage him to write and solve number sentences for each problem. Your youngsters will look forward to seeing their names as part of story problems and will be eager to solve them!

Diana Phillips—Gr. K
Murrayville-Woodson
  Elementary
Murraryville, IL

Guess the Missing Number and Win!

1	2	3	4	5	6	7	8	9	10
11	12	13	14	15	16		18	19	20
21	22	23	24	25	26	27	28	29	30
31	32	33	34	35	36	37	38	39	40
41	42	43	44	45	46	47	48	49	50
51	52	53	54	55	56	57	58	59	60
61	62	63	64	65	66	67			70
71	72	73	74	75	76	77			
81	82	83	84	85	86				
91	92	93	94	95	96				

Grant's dad raises pigs. Grant helped his dad put the pigs in a pen. There were three black pigs and two spotted pigs. How many pigs were there all together?

103

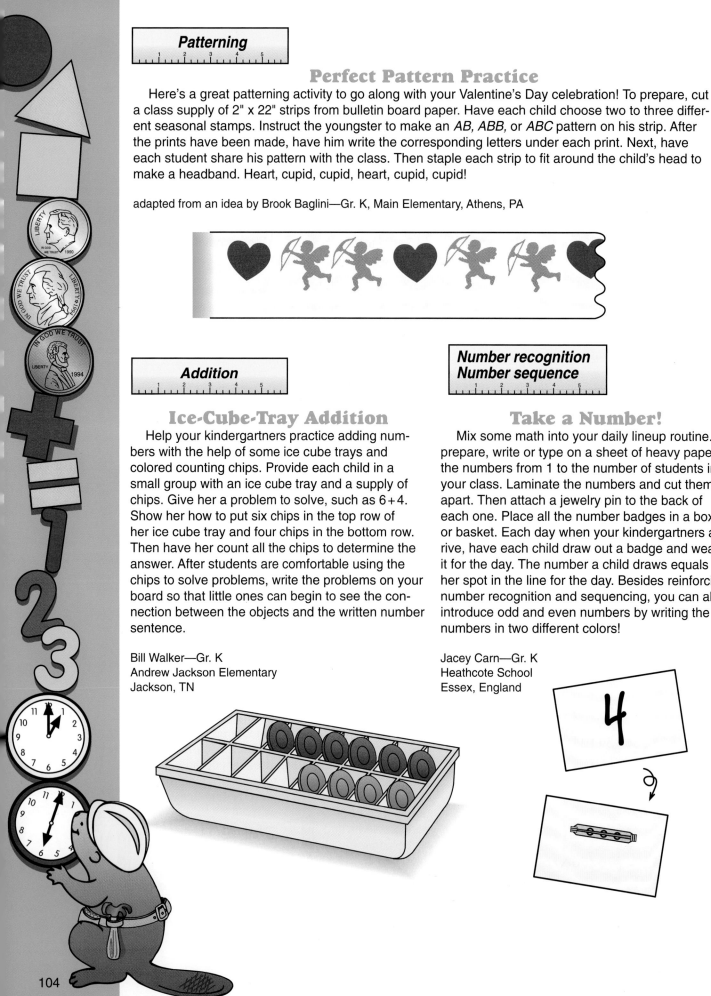

Patterning

Perfect Pattern Practice

Here's a great patterning activity to go along with your Valentine's Day celebration! To prepare, cut a class supply of 2" x 22" strips from bulletin board paper. Have each child choose two to three different seasonal stamps. Instruct the youngster to make an *AB, ABB,* or *ABC* pattern on his strip. After the prints have been made, have him write the corresponding letters under each print. Next, have each student share his pattern with the class. Then staple each strip to fit around the child's head to make a headband. Heart, cupid, cupid, heart, cupid, cupid!

adapted from an idea by Brook Baglini—Gr. K, Main Elementary, Athens, PA

Addition

Ice-Cube-Tray Addition

Help your kindergartners practice adding numbers with the help of some ice cube trays and colored counting chips. Provide each child in a small group with an ice cube tray and a supply of chips. Give her a problem to solve, such as 6+4. Show her how to put six chips in the top row of her ice cube tray and four chips in the bottom row. Then have her count all the chips to determine the answer. After students are comfortable using the chips to solve problems, write the problems on your board so that little ones can begin to see the connection between the objects and the written number sentence.

Bill Walker—Gr. K
Andrew Jackson Elementary
Jackson, TN

Number recognition
Number sequence

Take a Number!

Mix some math into your daily lineup routine. To prepare, write or type on a sheet of heavy paper the numbers from 1 to the number of students in your class. Laminate the numbers and cut them apart. Then attach a jewelry pin to the back of each one. Place all the number badges in a box or basket. Each day when your kindergartners arrive, have each child draw out a badge and wear it for the day. The number a child draws equals her spot in the line for the day. Besides reinforcing number recognition and sequencing, you can also introduce odd and even numbers by writing the numbers in two different colors!

Jacey Carn—Gr. K
Heathcote School
Essex, England

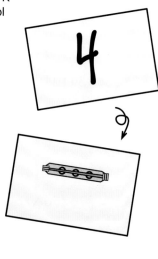

"Bag" to School!

Help ease your little ones' first-day jitters by welcoming each child to school with her own schoolhouse bag. To begin, glue on red construction paper to cover about two-thirds of the front of a paper lunch bag (as shown). Next, fold down the top of the bag and glue on a construction paper roof and bell. Use markers and additional construction paper pieces to add details to the schoolhouse. Then use a paint pen to label the roof with a student's name. Place a few school-related items inside the bag, such as an eraser, a pencil, and a bookmark. Position each bag in a child's chair or on her table space. What a wonderful schoolhouse welcome!

Dawn Schollenberger—Gr. K
Mary S. Shoemaker School
Woodstown, NJ

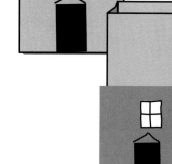

Kid Quotes

Use this idea to create a keepsake parents will cherish. To prepare, make a booklet for each child with one page for every month of the school year. Program each page with a different question such as the following: What makes you laugh? What do you want to be when you grow up? What makes you special? Once a month, have each child answer one of the questions from her booklet. Write her response on the page; then invite her to illustrate her answer. At the end of the school year, send the booklets home for parents to enjoy.

Marcia Snarski—Four- and Five-Year-Olds
St. Paul's Childhood Center
St. Paul, MN

Christmas Keepsake

Christmas probably isn't on the minds of most parents as they leave their little ones on the first day of school. However, every parent will treasure a Christmas ornament that displays a picture of her child on that monumental day. On the first day of school, take a photograph of each child in your class. Later, mount the picture on a cute construction paper cutout. Label the cutout similar to the one shown; then laminate it. Finally, punch a hole in the top of the cutout; then thread a length of yarn through it. What a way to light up a tree!

Susan Schneider—Gr. K
Durham Elementary School
Durham, NY

First Day of Kindergarten

September 5, 2003

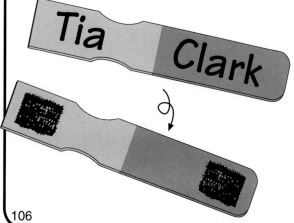

Portable Desktags

Changing your classroom seating is a breeze when you use these portable desktags! Ask a local paint store to donate a class supply of paint stirring sticks. Spray-paint the sticks; then use a permanent marker to label each one with a different child's name. Next, attach the hook side of a piece of self-adhesive Velcro fastener to each end of the stick. Attach the corresponding loop side to a student's desk or table. Then stick the desktag in place! These portable tags can easily be moved as you regroup students for various activities.

To reinforce the children's first and last names, paint the two halves of the sticks two different colors.

Rachel LeMarbe—Gr. K
Beaumont Elementary, Waterford, MI

Textured Turkey

Your youngsters will strut right in with their contributions for this class turkey project. To begin, cut a turkey body from brown paper and staple it to your bulletin board. Give each child a tagboard turkey feather to take home and cover with small decorative items, such as rice, cotton balls, or yarn. On a designated day, have children return their completed feathers to school; then invite them to touch and feel the different textures. Staple the feathers behind the turkey's body to form a tail. One look at this friendly fowl and students will know it's turkey time!

Connie Allen—Gr. K, Immanuel Lutheran School, Manitowoc, WI

Picture This!

Recycle clear film canisters into keepsakes with this ornament idea. To make a snowman, use a pushpin to poke a hole in the center of the lid. Straighten half of a paper clip, push it through the hole in the lid, and then bend the end, as shown. Paint the canister with craft glue and roll it in iridescent glitter. Snap the lid onto the canister. Make earmuffs by gluing the end of a three-inch pipe cleaner and a small pom-pom to each side. After the glue dries, use fabric paint to create the snowman's face. Voilá—a snowman to hang on your favorite limb!

adapted from an idea
  by Mary E. Maurer
Caddo, OK

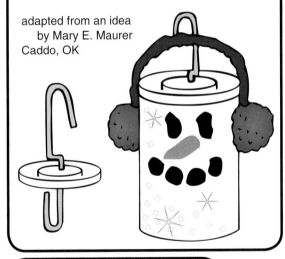

Rainmaker

Rain, rain, come today! This easy-to-make prop adds atmosphere and interest to any story about rain. It also makes a great addition to your water table supplies. To make a rainmaker, rinse an empty dishwashing-liquid bottle. Use a pushpin to poke about ten holes in the bottom of it. Fill the bottle with water; then screw the lid on and close the stopper. When you're sharing a rainy story, keep the rainmaker and an aluminum baking pan on hand. When you read a rainy part of the story, pull up the stopper and let it rain!

Jennifer Barton—Gr. K
Elizabeth Green School
Newington, CT

Spooky Counting

Youngsters will eat up this ghoulish counting activity! To begin, help each child trace both of his hands onto green construction paper. Then have him cut out the hand shapes. Direct him to glue the cutouts onto a sheet of purple construction paper; then have him glue one candy corn to the tip of each finger to resemble fingernails. When the glue is dry, have him count the fingers and then write a different number from 1 to 10 above each finger. When the child completes his paper, reward him with a handful of candy corn.

Gina G. Carter—Gr. K
Lebo St. Augustine School
Lebanon, KY

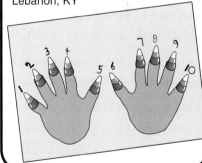

Ready for the Hall

Prepare youngsters for a quiet walk down the hall by having them chant the following rhyme:

My arms are by my side.
I'm standing nice and tall.
My eyes are looking straight ahead.
I'm ready for the hall!

Carrie Richardson—Gr. K
Dr. S. A. Mudd Elementary
Waldorf, MO

Sign, Please

This attendance book starts a daily routine that allows children to see their progress in writing their names. Ahead of time, use individual photos to make a supply of sign-in sheets similar to the one shown. Each morning, date one of the sheets and place it by the door. Have each youngster find her photo and sign her name beside it. Store the completed sheets in a notebook. During conference time, the notebook is a handy way to show a part of each student's development. She's on the "write" track!

Mary Beth Heath—Gr. K, Murrells Inlet, SC

107

Hit the Spot With Dot-to-Dot

Need a numeral sequencing center idea? These large dot-to-dots hit the spot! To make one, use an opaque projector to project a dot-to-dot picture on a large sheet of bulletin board paper. Trace the picture and numerals; then place a sticker dot on each dot in the picture. Laminate the picture. To use this dot-to-dot, post it on a wall or board and keep a supply of dry-erase markers and a cloth nearby. After you check a child's work, ask him to erase it so that the picture is ready for the next child who visits that center.

Tammy Riché—Gr. K, Kaplan Elementary, Kaplan, LA

Fingerpainting Fun

Here's a little twist on the fingerpainting process that makes even the cleanup fun! Before each child paints, instruct her to cover her hands with inexpensive plastic sandwich bags. When she is finished painting, have the child or a friend simply pull the bags off and toss 'em!

Susan A. DeRiso—Gr. K Barrington, RI

Shimmer and Shine

Recycling concepts shine forth in this creative project. In advance, ask children to bring in shiny scraps of holiday gift wrap, ribbons, and bows. Also suggest that they save and bring in colorful, shiny candy wrappers. When you have a substantial collection, give each child a piece of cardboard or tagboard to use as a base. Then invite each child to mix, match, twist, tie, cut, and glue to make his own original shimmery, shiny collage.

Elouise Miller—Gr. K
Lincoln School, Hays, KS

It's You!

Fine-tune youngsters' listening and vocabulary skills with this fun activity. Whenever you need to announce the name of an individual person, make statements that encourage students to figure out for themselves who that person is. For example, you might have your entire class stand and respond as you say the following: "Our helper today is a female." (All boys sit down.) "Our helper today is wearing horizontal stripes." (Discuss. All girls not wearing horizontal stripes sit down.) "Our helper today has pierced ears." When one person is left standing, the whole class says, "It's [child's name]!

Kathy Ramey—Gr. K
Hendron/Lone Oak Elementary
Paducah, KY

ABC...Look at Me!

Here's a snappy student display that focuses on letter recognition and phonemic awareness. Mount an alphabet line on a wall at your children's eye level. Take a photo of each child holding a sentence strip with his name printed on it. Next, tape each child's photo above the first letter of his first name. Then, after the winter holidays, put the picture above the first letter of his last name. In a flash, your children will become familiar with the letters and sounds of their own names and their classmates' names too!

Robbin Williams—Gr. K
Montclair Elementary
Orange Park, FL

How Do You Feel Today?

Help your children learn to verbalize their feelings and, in the process, you'll get to know your students better! Begin by programming a sentence strip with "How do you feel today?" Gather pictures that convey emotions. Glue each picture to a different tagboard card and label the card with the corresponding emotion. Next, write each child's name on a different tagboard card. Attach magnetic strips to the back of each piece. Then arrange the title question and emotion pictures on a magnetic board (as shown). Keep the name cards nearby. To use this activity, have each child find his name and place it next to the emotion that shows how he is feeling at that time. Lots of good discussion starters here!

Catherine Carlisle
Buckeye Wood
   Elementary
Grove City, OH

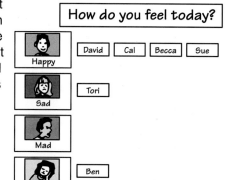

Glitter Catcher

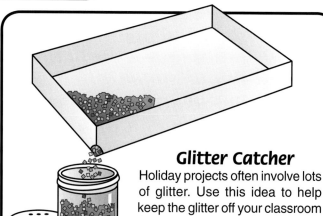

Holiday projects often involve lots of glitter. Use this idea to help keep the glitter off your classroom floor! Cut a hole in one corner of a shallow cardboard box, such as a soda can box, or the lid of a larger box. Place an art project in the box and sprinkle glitter over it. When the project is dry, shake it over the box to remove any excess glitter. Then pour the excess glitter through the hole in the box and back into a container. Glitter be gone!

Amy Massa—Gr. K
Tuttle Elementary
Sarasota, FL

108

Have a Seat on That...Placemat?

Yes! Durable vinyl placemats in fun shapes will help little ones keep their seats during circle time. Purchase a class supply of placemats in cute shapes, such as bears and fish. Place one on the carpet where you'd like each child to sit. Then invite youngsters to find a seat. Neat!

Cathie Rubley Hart—Gr. K
Westwood Hills Elementary
Waynesboro, VA

The Be-Quiet Bee

Call on some cute and cuddly critters to help groups of youngsters remember to keep quiet while you are assessing individual students. A stuffed bee, known as the Be-Quiet Bee, can land on a quiet table, but it might flit away if the noise level gets too high! You might also try a Whisper Whale, a Bashful Bear, or a Gentle Giraffe. You'll be surprised how hard youngsters work to keep these quiet pals around!

Michele Galvan—Gr. K, Roosevelt Elementary, McAllen, TX

Whisper, Whisper...Shout!

Here's a fun way to reinforce months of the year and days of the week. Each day at calendar time, have your class whisper the days of the week in order. But when you reach the current day, have them shout it out! Do the same when reciting the months of the year, shouting out only the current month. Kindergartners love having permission to shout indoors, and the repetition of this activity will reinforce these important calendar concepts.

Wendy Rivilis—K4 and K5; ABC Kids Care, Inc.; Grafton, WI

I Pledge!

If your class is learning the Pledge of Allegiance, here's a motivational display just for you! First, cover a board with red bulletin board paper. Cut out the title's letters from white construction paper. Glue each letter to a different blue circle; then mount the title on the board. As each child learns the Pledge of Allegiance, write her name on a white star cutout and help her staple it onto the lower portion of the board. Now that's allegiance!

Betsy Ruggiano, Featherbed Lane School, Clark, NJ

Rainbow Writing

Do your St. Patrick's Day shenanigans include a visit from a mysterious leprechaun? Have the tricky fellow replace all your students' standard pencils with colored pencils for a day! You'll soon see a rainbow of writing!

Donna Spanarellii—Gr. K
Roberge School
River Vale, NJ

Scissor Savvy

When glue accumulates on your students' safety scissors, take them home and run them through your dishwasher. They'll be as good as new and shiny too!

Lisa Smith—Gr. K
Albany Elementary
Albany, KY

Bunny Booklet

Your youngsters will be celebrating the season with these adorable accordion-folded booklets! To make one, cut six egg shapes from white tagboard; then use clear tape to attach them in one long strip. Have each child accordion-fold the strip, glue on two long ears, and then decorate the cover to resemble a bunny face complete with a pom-pom nose. Help her add her name and "Bunnies" to the cover. Have her unfold the booklet and program the pages as shown. Instruct her to make yellow paint fingerprints, as shown, on each page and then use a fine-tip marker to transform each one into a bunny. On the last page, simply add ears to each bunny and glue on a white dot made with a hole puncher for each tail. Finally, glue a cotton ball to the back of the booklet for a cute bunny tail!

Lucia Kemp Henry
Fallon, NV

One bunny. Two bunnies. Three bunnies. Four bunnies. Runaway bunnies!

Names, Please!

Use this song to remind your kindergartners to write their names on their papers. Challenge them to have their pages labeled by the time you finish singing.

(sung to the tune of "Do Your Ears Hang Low?")

Can you write your name?
Can you write it nice and neat?
Will you please sign your paper
Before you leave your seat?
It's a simple thing to do.
And it lets me know you're through.
Can you write your name?

adapted from a song by Laura Butts—Gr. K
Thorndale Elementary, Thorndale, TX

Hands Are for Helping

Are you often reminding your students to keep their hands and feet to themselves? Put a positive spin on that message by saying, "Hands are for helping!" When a child touches something or someone she shouldn't, ask, "What are hands for?" Have the student answer, "Hands are for helping." You'll soon see students reminding one another of this concept when peer conflicts arise.

Jean Ricotta—Lead Teacher
Signal Hill Elementary
Dix Hills, NY

Higher and Higher...

Which cone's scoop will rise the highest? Your students will be the judges of that! In advance, cut out three construction paper cones. Label one "chocolate," one "strawberry," and one "vanilla." Slice a rectangular half gallon of Neapolitan ice cream so that each child will have a bit of each flavor to taste. After tasting, have each child cut out a construction paper scoop of ice cream in the color of the flavor she liked best. Have each child say the name of her favorite flavor and then tape her scoop on the corresponding cone. When this graph is complete, you'll have scoops of opportunities to reinforce *more, less,* and *equal.*

Jennifer Barton—Gr. K
Elizabeth Green School
Newington, CT

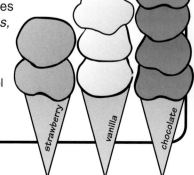

strawberry vanilla chocolate

And Cupcakes for All!

How can you make sure every child gets to celebrate her birthday with her classmates? Make a request on your school supplies list. Along with scissors and glue, ask each parent to send in a box of cake mix and a container of frosting. (For those who are unable to contribute, you may need to furnish several boxes or ask a few parents to send in extras.) Then make cupcakes for the class on each student's birthday. Summer birthdays can be celebrated as half-birthdays (a July 10 birthday would be celebrated on January 10) or at the end of the school year. Now *that's* fair!

Joyce Wilkerson—Grs. PreK–K
Jefferson Elementary
Sherman, TX

Theme Units

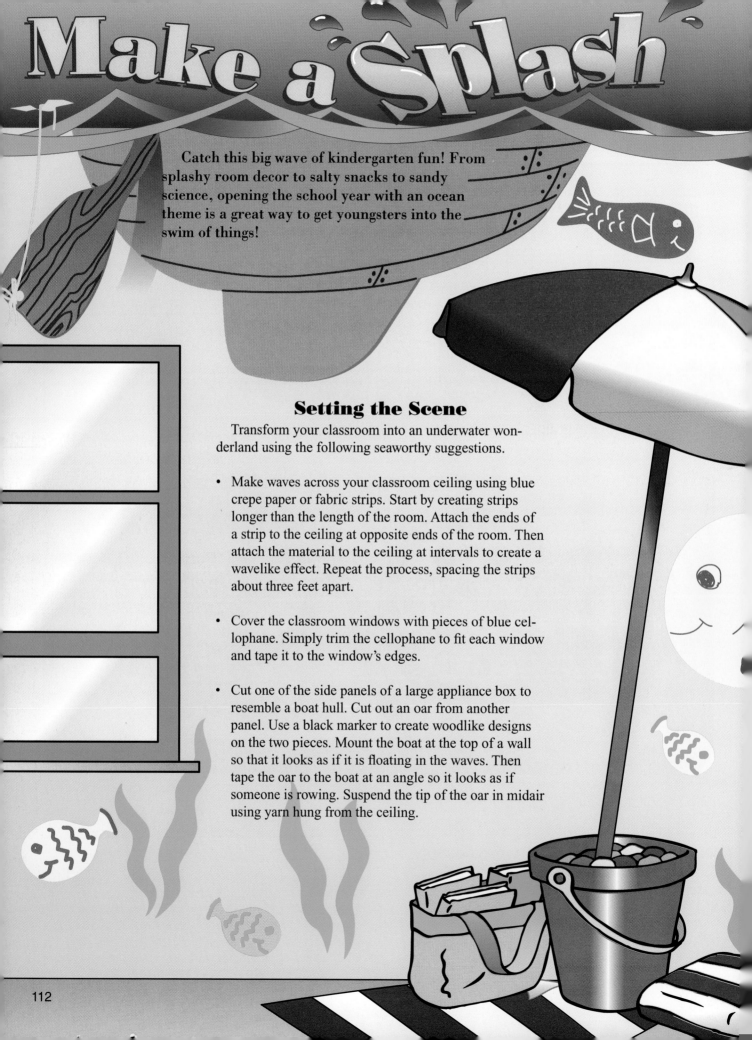

Make a Splash

Catch this big wave of kindergarten fun! From splashy room decor to salty snacks to sandy science, opening the school year with an ocean theme is a great way to get youngsters into the swim of things!

Setting the Scene

Transform your classroom into an underwater wonderland using the following seaworthy suggestions.

- Make waves across your classroom ceiling using blue crepe paper or fabric strips. Start by creating strips longer than the length of the room. Attach the ends of a strip to the ceiling at opposite ends of the room. Then attach the material to the ceiling at intervals to create a wavelike effect. Repeat the process, spacing the strips about three feet apart.

- Cover the classroom windows with pieces of blue cellophane. Simply trim the cellophane to fit each window and tape it to the window's edges.

- Cut one of the side panels of a large appliance box to resemble a boat hull. Cut out an oar from another panel. Use a black marker to create woodlike designs on the two pieces. Mount the boat at the top of a wall so that it looks as if it is floating in the waves. Then tape the oar to the boat at an angle so it looks as if someone is rowing. Suspend the tip of the oar in midair using yarn hung from the ceiling.

in Kindergarten

- Embellish your walls with a variety of fish cut from fluorescent poster board. Use fluorescent paints to create designs on the fish. Then attach them at various heights on the walls. They'll seem to glow in the blue light. As an added touch, attach cutouts of green poster board seaweed for the fish to hide in and swim around.

- Ready your reading center for fun in the sun! Secure a beach umbrella in a large sand bucket filled with sand or rocks. Spread out several beach towels under the umbrella. Then stock the center with a few beach bags filled with ocean-related literature.

- Set up this discovery center for exploring seashells. Fill a kiddie pool with a couple of inches of sand; then bury a variety of shells. Provide several shovels and place some shell reference books nearby to assist students in their sandy adventures.

Monica D. Raymer
Gavin Cochran Elementary
Louisville, KY

Dive Into Kindergarten

This inviting door decor will welcome your new students and immediately make them feel like a part of your school. Cover your classroom door with blue paper; then attach a welcoming cutout. Prepare fish-shaped nametags and attach them to the door so that they can be removed and worn.

As youngsters arrive on the first day of school, have each child find his nametag, remove it from the door, and replace it with his decorated fish from "Cast a Net" on page 114. Splish, splash!

Donna Battista
Parkview Elementary
Valparaiso, IN

Cast a Net

Use a welcome letter as your net to gather your little fishies together for the first day of school. About a week before school starts, send each of your new students a letter on ocean-themed stationery. In the letter, introduce yourself, tell about exciting activities that the child will get to experience, and let the child know how to find you on the first day (see "Here I Am!" below). If possible, put a photograph in the letter to help the child start to put your face with your name. Finally, include in the letter a tagboard cutout of a fish. Instruct each child and her family to decorate the fish any way they wish. Remind them to include the child's name somewhere on the front of the fish. Encourage the child to bring her fish to school on the first day to help you decorate the classroom. (See "Dive Into Kindergarten" on page 113.) What a catch!

Donna Battista
Parkview Elementary
Valparaiso, IN

Here I Am!

Be easy to spot on the first day of school! Use some of the props listed below to help your new students instantly recognize you. In your welcome letter (see "Cast a Net" above), tell youngsters what to look for. Then don your gear on the first day and watch for big smiles!

Possible props:

sunglasses	sun hat
mask and snorkel	captain's hat
flippers	sailor suit
beach-print clothing	beach bag
wet suit	beach towel (wear around your neck
inner tube or swim ring	or over your shoulders)
boogie board	sand shoes
sandals or flip-flops	sand pail or shovel

adapted from an idea by Sylvie Audet-Faddis
Arthur Robinson P.S.
Sudbury, Ontario, Canada

My New Friends

Help youngsters introduce themselves to one another with this neat sticker exchange. Ahead of time, use a computer printing program to create ocean-themed personalized stickers for each child. Print enough copies of each child's design so that he'll be able to give one to each of his classmates. Laminate a sheet of construction paper for each child. Use a permanent marker to label each sheet "Friends I Met at School." As youngsters mingle on the first day, encourage them to exchange stickers and stick their friends' names on their pages. Parents will also appreciate having names to talk about with their children.

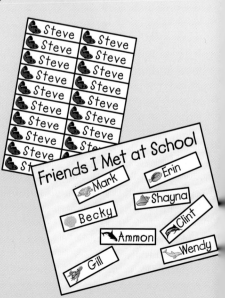

Sandra Stone-Husocki—Gr. K
Boca, FL

114

Name Game

Play this fishy game during one of your first circle times to help students learn their classmates' names. All you need for the game is a small stuffed fish toy. To begin, toss the fish to a child as you lead the group in chanting, "Fishy, fishy, in the sea, won't you share your name with me?" Invite the chosen child to say her name aloud; then have everyone else say, "Welcome aboard, [child's name]!" For the next round, direct the child to toss the fish to another classmate and begin the chant again. Continue until each youngster has had a turn to catch and toss. It's nice to meet you!

Donna Battista
Parkview Elementary
Valparaiso, IN

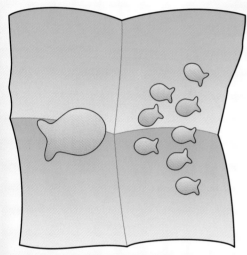

Just Like the Story!

Leo Lionni's friendship and teamwork messages in *Swimmy* are perfect for a beginning-of-the-year ocean unit. After sharing the story with your little ones and discussing its moral, work on some comprehension and recall skills. Give each child one giant Goldfish cracker and a handful of the original Goldfish crackers. (If desired, add one pretzel Goldfish cracker to represent Swimmy.) Each child will also need a blue napkin.

Direct each youngster to unfold his napkin to make an ocean. Then, as you reread the story, encourage the child to use the crackers to act it out. Once the story is over, the snacking can begin.

Donna Battista

A Sea Song

Add some music and movement to your deep-sea welcome with this fun tune. After your youngsters catch on, encourage them to create more verses and motions.

(sung to the tune of "The Wheels on the Bus")

The fish in the ocean go swish, swish, swish,
Swish, swish, swish,
Swish, swish, swish.
The fish in the ocean go swish, swish, swish
All through the sea!

Make swimming motions with arms and hands.

The lobsters…snip, snip, snip
The sharks…chomp, chomp, chomp

Make pinching motions with fingers.
With one forearm on top of the other,
  make clapping motions with hands.

The skates…flap, flap, flap
The crabs…skit, scat, skit

Move arms in slow, flying motions.
Run in place.

Susan Daley
Narragansett Elementary School
Warwick, RI

Pizza, Please!

Are you hungry for a cross-curricular unit that students will eat up? October is National Pizza Month, so why not try these fresh, hot pizza ideas? Any way you slice it, little ones will be learning!

Sing a Song of Pizza

Mouths will be watering when you slice into your pizza study with this song and activity! To prepare, decorate five tagboard circles to resemble pizzas. On the back of each circle, write a different letter found in the word *pizza*. To begin the activity, have five children line up and face the class. Give each of the five students a tagboard circle. Have the students hold up the letters to spell *pizza*. Next, invite your class to sing the adaption of "Bingo" to the right. Sing the song a second time and omit the letter *P*. Direct the child holding that letter to turn his circle and show the pizza instead. Continue singing until all the letters have been turned.

Angela Van Beveren—Gr. K
E. C. Mason Elementary, Alvin, TX

P-I-Z-Z-A
(sung to the tune of "Bingo")

There is a treat we love to eat,
And pizza is its name, oh!
P-I-Z-Z-A! P-I-Z-Z-A! P-I-Z-Z-A!
And pizza is its name, oh!

Toss in Some Toppings!

This gross-motor activity is the tops! In advance, obtain a parachute or a large flat bedsheet. Cut a variety of pizza toppings from felt, such as cheese, pepperoni, olives, and mushrooms. Have students hold the edges of the sheet and pretend it is a giant pizza crust. Invite them to gently shake the sheet up and down as they sing the song below. Each time a new topping is mentioned, add the felt topping to the sheet for students to toss.

(sung to the tune of "Old MacDonald")

Oh, let's make a pizza pie, P-I-Z-Z-A!
And on that pie we'll put some [cheese].
P-I-Z-Z-A!
We're making it fresh! We're making it hot!
Make it fresh! Make it hot! And then we'll eat a whole lot!
Oh, let's make a pizza pie, P-I-Z-Z-A!

Repeat the song, replacing the underlined word with other popular pizza toppings.

Angela Van Beveren—Gr. K

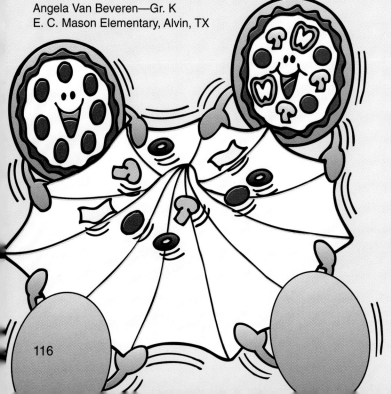

Pass the Pizza

Reinforce letter, shape, or number recognition with this lively game. In advance, create a desired number of construction paper pizzas. Program the middle of each pizza with a letter, shape, or number; then place the pizzas in an unused pizza box. To play the game, have students sit in a circle and pass the pizza box while singing the song below. When the song ends, direct the child holding the box to open it and identify the symbol on the top pizza. Then have him take the pizza out, close the box, and begin passing it again. Pass the pizza, please.

(sung to the tune of "Pop Goes the Weasel")

Pass the pizza round a bit.
Can you name who will get it?
Delivered hot, right to the spot!
Oh! It's [name of child holding the box]!

Rachel Meseke Castro, Castro's Kids, Albuquerque, NM

Fraction Action

Introduce your youngsters to the basics of fractions with this mouthwatering manipulative. In advance, collect ads with color photographs of pizza. Then cut out eight tagboard circles. Program four of the circles similar to those shown. Next, glue the pizza photos to the four remaining circles to create realistic pizza collages. Cut one pizza in half, one in thirds, and one in fourths. Keep one pizza whole. Set the tagboard circles and pizza pieces at a center. Then invite each child to visit the center and match the pizza slices with the fractions on the circles.

Kathy Thomure, Raytown, MO

Pizza Paintings

These scented pizza paintings smell good enough to eat! To make one, cut a sheet of paper to fit the bottom of a round, nonstick pizza pan. Set the paper aside and invite a child to paint the bottom of the pan to resemble a pizza. Next, direct the child to carefully press the paper on the pan to make a pizza print. Have her remove the paper from the pan and then sprinkle a little garlic powder and oregano on the wet paint. When the paint is dry, mount a red-and-white-checkered tablecloth on a bulletin board; then add a title and each child's pizza to the display. Presto! Pizza prints that look and smell good enough to eat!

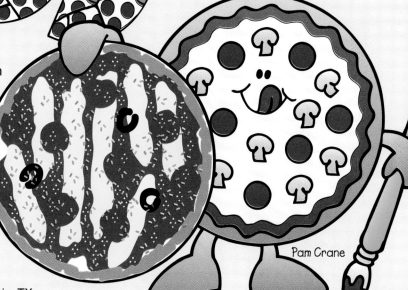

Angela Van Beveren—Gr. K, E. C. Mason Elementary, Alvin, TX

117

Make a Pizza

A variety of math and reading skills will be delivered right to your little ones with this center idea! In advance, prepare a set of pizza recipe cards similar to the ones shown. Then cut out several pizza crusts and toppings from felt. Place the cards and felt shapes at a center. Invite each child to choose a card and then use the felt pieces to create a pizza according to the recipe. When your little pizza chef has completed the center, reward him with a handful of pizza-flavored crackers. Oh, mama mia!

Lynn C. Mode—Gr. K
Benton Heights Elementary
Monroe, NC

1 brown crust
red sauce
3 black olives
5 red pepperoni slices

1 brown crust
red sauce
2 brown mushrooms
4 green pepper slices

Sorting Slices

Your youngsters will have all sorts of fun with this classification idea! To prepare, photocopy the pizza pattern on page 119. Use a black marker to draw different toppings or numbers of toppings on each slice. Then make three or four copies of the completed pizza. Color the pizzas. Laminate them and then cut out each slice. Place the slices in a clean, empty pizza box and invite students to sort the slices by toppings, number of toppings, or shape of toppings. What a supreme pizza idea!

Shawna L. Punch, R. Cage Elementary, Houston, TX

That's a Lotto Pizza!

Spice up letter recognition with this saucy lotto game! To prepare, duplicate the pizza pattern on page 119 to make a class supply of slices. Program each slice with a different set of letters; then laminate and cut out each slice. To play the game, provide each child with a programmed pizza slice and some red bingo chips (pepperoni). As you call out letters, have each child use the chips to cover the matching letters on her card. When all of her letters are covered, direct her to say, "Pizza!"

Rachel Meseke Castro, Castro's Kids, Albuquerque, NM

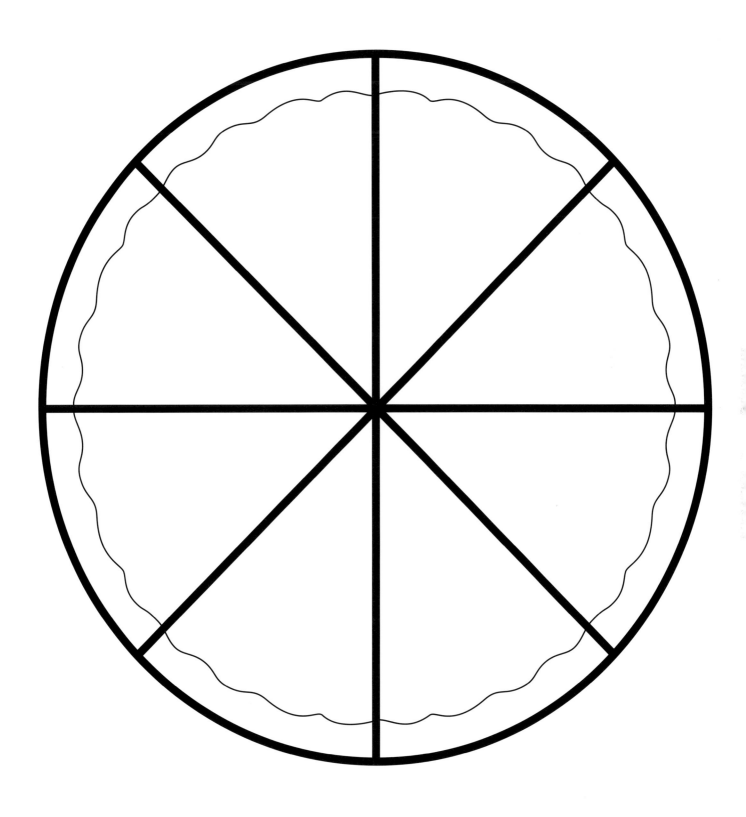

Thanksgiving

Thanksgiving is a time for friends, family, food, and fun. But it's also a time to remember our long-celebrated Thanksgiving friends—the Pilgrims and Native Americans. Use the ideas in this unit to teach your youngsters about the history of one of our most beloved American holidays.

ideas contributed by Allison Ward

Telling the Tale

The story leading up to the very first Thanksgiving is certainly a tale worth telling! Share the history of Thanksgiving with your children by reading Ann McGovern's *The Pilgrims' First Thanksgiving*. The simple text and realistic illustrations introduce youngsters to the trials and triumphs leading up to that historic day. If this title isn't available, see the list of additional realistic-fiction books below. Then tell the tale!

Across the Wide Dark Sea
Written by Jean Van Leeuwen
Illustrated by Thomas B. Allen

On the Mayflower
Written by Kate Waters
Photographs by Russ Kendall

The Story of the Pilgrims
Written by Katharine Ross
Illustrated by Carolyn Croll

Three Young Pilgrims
Written & illustrated by Cheryl Harness

The Mayflower

Making a Mayflower

Hoist the sails on creativity as children design a rich dramatic-play experience. After sharing the story of the first Thanksgiving (see "Telling the Tale"), invite small groups of children to share in creating a classroom *Mayflower*. Begin with a large box. Encourage groups of children to paint the outside of the box to resemble the *Mayflower*. (Keep your collection of Thanksgiving books handy for children's reference.) Then encourage student groups to use art supplies to create the ship's details (see the illustration). This ship will launch youngsters on hours of Thanksgiving dramatic play!

Jennifer Miller—Grs. K–1 Special Education, Alann Elementary School, Reston, VA

Mayflower Menu

Mealtime on the *Mayflower* was no picnic—so to speak! Since there was no refrigeration on the ship, the Pilgrims had to bring food that would not spoil during the long journey. Give your youngsters just a sampling of *Mayflower* fare. When you share another realistic Thanksgiving book, serve your children beef jerky, hard cheese, and crackers. Invite each child to snack on these *Mayflower* foods while you read. Afterward, ask children for their comments. Not bad for a day or two? How about 66 days?

Remembered

Packing Pilgrims

What would you take to a brand-new land if you were traveling on a very crowded ship? Pose this question to your children, reminding them that the Pilgrims were going to a land where there would be no refrigerators, houses, or stores. In fact, they were going to a wilderness! Encourage each child to imagine that she is a Pilgrim and illustrate one thing that she would pack to bring on the ship. (If desired, suggest realistic ideas from the list below.) Then have each child cut out her illustration and glue it to the inside of your classroom *Mayflower*. By the way, did you know that one *Mayflower* passenger brought along 126 pairs of shoes? Of course, he shared!

On Board the Ship

sacks of cabbages, turnips, dried peas, flour	tools
barrels of salted meat, smoked fish	books
rounds of cheese	farm animals
seeds	two dogs
gardening tools	one cat
cookware	

Jennifer Miller—Grs. K–1 Special Education

Ship Shape

With a little creative artistry, these *Mayflower* look-alikes take on fine form. To make one ship, photocopy the ship pattern (page 124) on brown construction paper. Cut out the pattern; then place it on a large sheet of blue paper. Arrange one end each of three craft sticks behind the ship (to resemble masts). Next, cut out an assortment of sail shapes from paper, wallpaper, or fabric scraps. Then glue all the pieces in place. Use these ships for the activity described in "What's in a Name?"

What's in a Name?

Most researchers think that the *Mayflower* was named after the pretty white flower that grows on the hawthorn tree and blooms in May in England. These researchers also think that there was probably a picture of that flower painted on the *Mayflower*. After discussing this with your children, encourage each child to think of a meaningful name for her own ship (made in "Ship Shape"). Then have her draw a picture, cut it out, and glue it onto her ship. Also invite each child to use markers to add colorful details to her ship if desired. Then have each child hold her finished project and "sail" it in front of her as you all sing "Sail, Sail, Sail Our Ship" (on page 122). Then encourage youngsters to take their finished projects home and share the whole Thanksgiving story and song with their families.

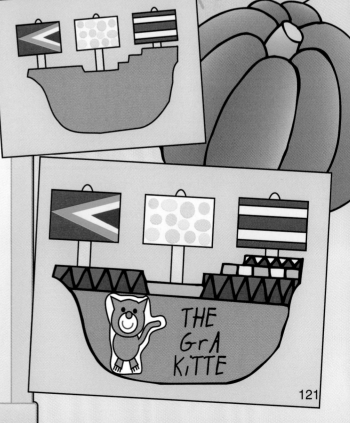

THE GrA KiTTE

Sail, Sail, Sail Our Ship

Here's a little sailing song that your pretend Pilgrims might like to sing as they journey at sea.

(sung to the tune of "Row, Row, Row Your Boat")

> Sail, sail, sail our ship
> Across the deep blue sea.
> We're sailing to America
> Where we can all be free.

Thanks, Squanto!

Corn chips, corn dogs, cornflakes, corn bread—where would we be without corn? And more to the Thanksgiving point, where would we be without Squanto? Squanto was a Native American who spoke English. After he met the Pilgrims, he decided to stay with them and help them survive in the new land. Among many other important things, Squanto taught the Pilgrims how to grow corn. Without this corn, the Pilgrims would have starved. So take a moment to recognize Squanto with this creatively corny art project. Stock your art area with colored and regular popcorn kernels, popped popcorn, tagboard pieces, and craft glue. Encourage each child in the center to squeeze a glue design onto a piece of tagboard. Then have him arrange the popped popcorn and the kernels along the glue lines. When the glue is dry, back each creation with another color of tagboard. Then mount all the projects on a board titled "Thanks, Squanto!" Encourage your little ones to share Squanto's story with classroom visitors.

Three Days of Thanks

After the Pilgrims' first very difficult winter in the new land, they were so thankful to be alive and to have a bountiful fall harvest that they celebrated for *three days in a row!* After explaining this to your youngsters, launch three days of thanks in your classroom. To prepare, cut out a large butcher-paper basket and mount it on a board titled "Thinking Thankful Thoughts." Then enlarge and duplicate a supply of the food patterns (page 125) on colorful construction paper. Prompt children to begin thinking about what they are thankful for in their lives. On the first of your chosen three days, have each child choose a food cutout and write or illustrate a thankful thought on it. Then help him mount it in the basket. Repeat this activity on the second and third days, creating an overflowing display of thankful thoughts.

Are Ye Ready? Are Ye Set?

Eating wasn't the only thing going on during that first Thanksgiving celebration—there were lots of fun and games too! Running races and tug-of-war are two activities that have held people's interest from way back then until now. This year when you take your youngsters out for a few running races and a couple rounds of tug-of-war, add a touch of the old days to the festivities. To start off each game or race, call out, "Are ye ready? Are ye set? Go!"

Pumpkin Delight

Although pumpkin pie is standard fare for Thanksgiving these days, historians think that the *pie* part might not have been around until a couple years after the very first Thanksgiving. So if you're planning to have a classroom feast, try adding this form of pumpkin to your menu. First, cut the top off a baking pumpkin. Then have your youngsters help remove the seeds and pulp. Next, fill the pumpkin with apple chunks, raisins, and cranberries. Sprinkle the filling with cinnamon and sugar, and dot with butter. Replace the pumpkin top and bake the pumpkin on a cookie sheet in a 350° oven for approximately 1½ hours. To serve, scoop out the warm fruit as well as the pumpkin. Mmm…delightful!

Pam Crane

I wd liK to milK a got.

I can sit down to eat.

Thanksgiving-Related Stories

1, 2, 3 Thanksgiving!
Written by W. Nikola-Lisa
Illustrated by Robin Kramer

Albert's Thanksgiving
Written & illustrated by Leslie Tryon

Thanksgiving Treat
Written & illustrated by Catherine Stock

Today Is Thanksgiving!
Written & illustrated by P. K. Hallinan

Thanksgiving at the Tappletons'
Written by Eileen Spinelli
Illustrated by Maryann Cocca-Leffler

Turkey Pox
Written by Laurie Halse Anderson
Illustrated by Dorothy Donohue

Looking Back

Get your modern-day pilgrims pondering the past with this thought-provoking activity. To set the stage, read aloud a book that realistically depicts life in the new land. Some especially good choices include *Sarah Morton's Day, Samuel Eaton's Day,* and *Tapenum's Day* by Kate Waters. Photographed in full color at Plimoth Plantation—a living history museum—these books accurately offer an up-close look at different children's days in 17th-century America.

After sharing the book(s), prompt your students to brainstorm a list of activities in which children participated in those early days. Write their comments on chart paper. Then give each child a large sheet of construction paper and ask her to fold it in half. On one half, encourage each child to write about and illustrate one thing from the past that she wishes she could do in the present. On the other half, have her illustrate one thing that she is happy she does not have to do now. Bind all the pages between construction paper covers with the title "Now & Then." Invite each child to share her page with the group. Ah, this is the life…or was *that?*

123

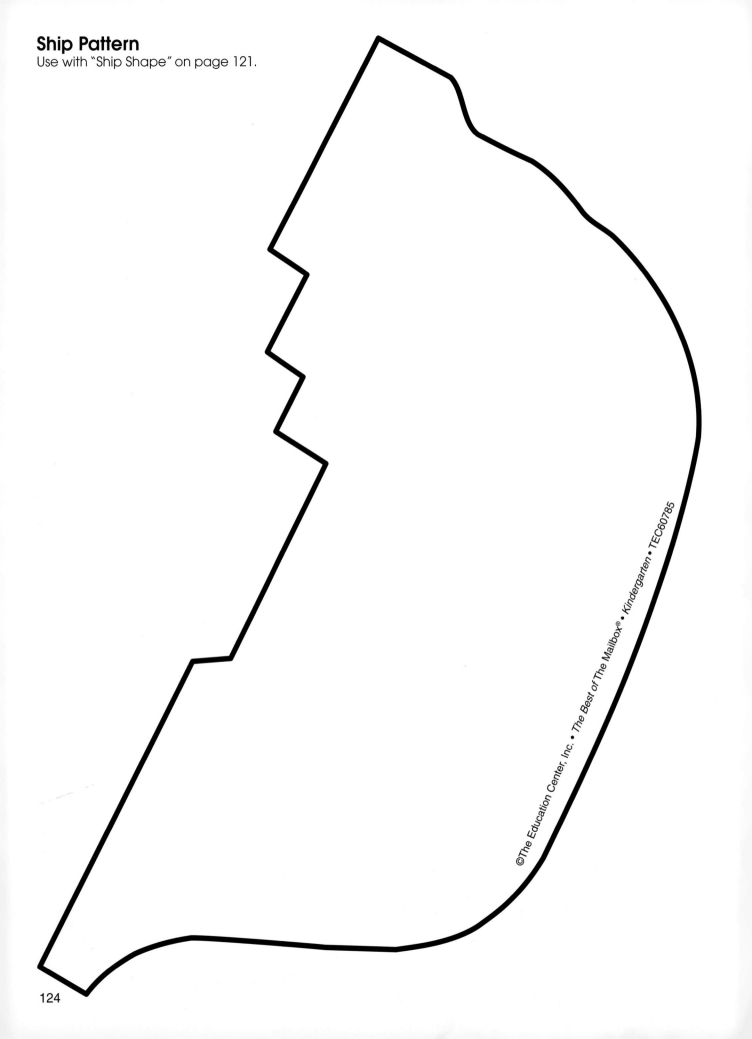

Ship Pattern
Use with "Ship Shape" on page 121.

©The Education Center, Inc. • The Best of The Mailbox® • Kindergarten • TEC60785

124

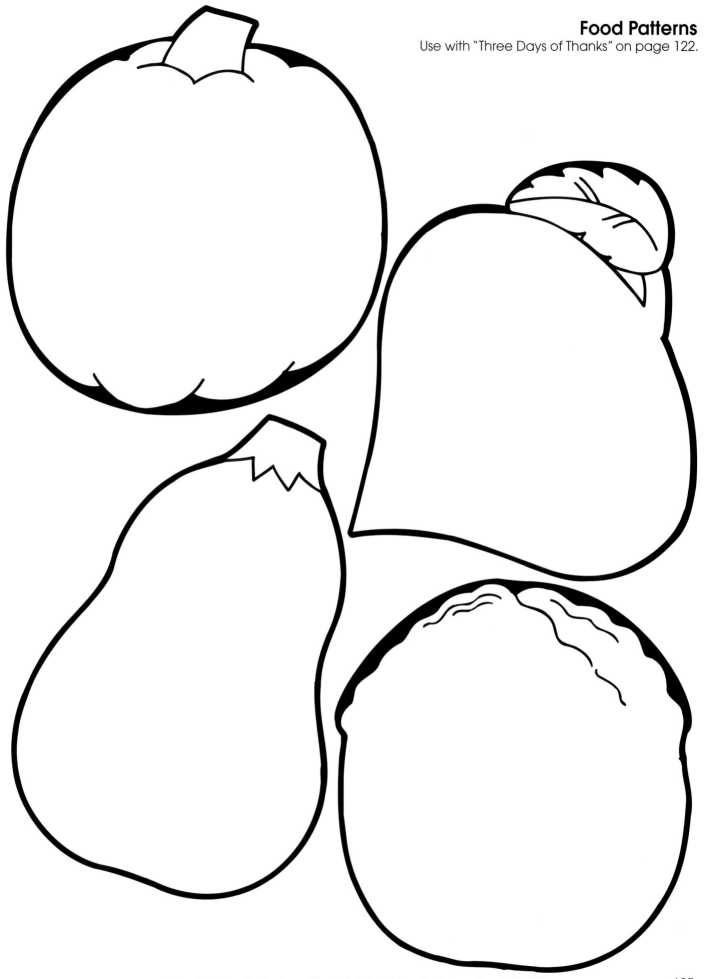

Special You, Special Me!

Snowflakes and children are both one of a kind. This blizzard of activities focuses on self-esteem and will help your youngsters *see* that to be *different* is to be *special*.

ideas contributed by Susan A. DeRiso, Carole Dibble, and Kathy Lee

A Special Sharing

Celebrate the uniqueness of each student during circle time with this special touch. In advance, create this snowflake wand using a sheet of one-inch-thick foam, a 12-inch wooden dowel, two wiggle eyes, and red felt. To make the wand, use a serrated knife to cut out a snowflake from the foam. If desired, use the pattern on page 129 as a template. Insert the dowel into the bottom of the snowflake to create a handle. Then glue on the wiggle eyes and a felt mouth as shown.

Have students pass the wand around the circle while singing the tune below. Encourage the child holding the wand at the end of the verse to share something special about himself. Continue singing the verse until each child has had a turn to share.

I'm Something Special

(sung to the tune of "London Bridge")

Share with us some special news,
Special news, special news.
Share with us some special news
About you!

Pam Crane

Fingerprinting Flurry

Frolicking fingers make a flurry of snow in this activity. Explain to your little ones that fingerprints and snowflakes are similar because there are no two flakes nor fingerprints that are exactly alike. Give each child a sheet of dark-colored construction paper and provide access to white washable paint. Demonstrate how to draw several lines on the paper that intersect at the same point. Encourage the child to use the lines as guides and make fingerprints (or use toes!) along and beside the lines to create her own unique snowflake. Cut out the flakes and display them together with the title "A Flurry of Fun!"

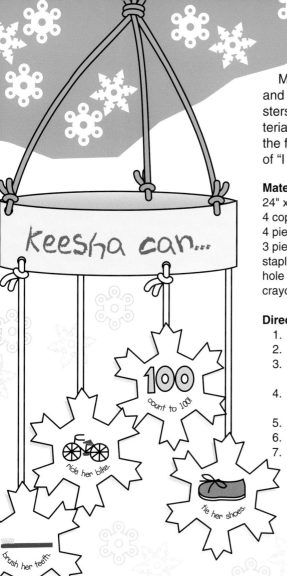

A Snowstorm of Successes

Many things make us unique. Often we are differentiated by things we can and cannot do. By focusing on the *cans* with this snowy mobile, your youngsters will be shoveling up mounds of self-esteem. Gather the necessary materials listed below. Then assist each child in completing the directions. Hang the finished mobiles from your ceiling to create a constant reminder of "I can!" Wow, there's a real feeling of success in the air!

Materials for each student:
24" x 3" tagboard strip
4 copies of the snowflake pattern on page 129
4 pieces of white yarn cut in different lengths
3 pieces of blue yarn cut the same length
stapler
hole puncher
crayons

Directions:
1. Write your name and "can…" on the tagboard strip.
2. Staple the ends of the strip together to form a cylinder.
3. Punch four holes around the bottom of the cylinder and three holes around the top.
4. On each snowflake, write/dictate and illustrate a different activity that you can complete successfully.
5. Cut out the snowflakes and then punch a hole at the top of each one.
6. Attach each snowflake to the bottom of the cylinder with a white piece of yarn.
7. Tie one end of each piece of blue yarn to a different hole in the top of the cylinder; then tie the loose ends together.

A Blizzard of Praise

Shake up spirits with these rewarding jars of praise. In advance, collect a class supply of clean baby food jars (with the labels removed). Also, duplicate and cut out the snowflake pattern below for each child.

To make a praise jar, cut a child's photo to fit the inside of the jar's lid. Then laminate the photo and hot-glue it to the inside of the lid. Next, fill the jar with water, add some silver glitter, and secure the lid. Finally, glue the snowflake to the top of the lid.

Keep the jars on students' desks or tables and use them as magical, motivating rewards. To give praise and attention to a deserving child, simply turn his jar upside down. Now *that's* something to cheer about!

Double the Pleasure, Double the Fun

This version of the traditional memory game gets up close and personal to help students refine their visual-discrimination skills. To prepare the game, duplicate the snowflake cards on page 130 on tagboard and then cut them apart. Make two copies of each child's photograph. Cut out the duplicated photos and mount them on the tagboard cards. Mix the cards together and arrange them facedown on a tabletop. (If there are too many cards, divide them to make two games.) Then invite each child in a small group to try to find a matching pair. Look carefully!

Pattern

Hooray for ME!

127

Snowflake Snacks

Your little ones will love creating these uniquely different treats. Gather the ingredients and supplies listed below. Have each child place part of a doily on top of her cupcake. Then help her sift powdered sugar over the doily. Carefully remove it to reveal a snowflake design. No two treats will be the same!

Materials needed:
chocolate cupcake per child
powdered sugar
sifter
doilies

If You Were a Snowflake...

Hmmm, what would you do? Youngsters will have no trouble pretending to be snowflakes in this creative-thinking activity. Duplicate page 131 for each child. Pose the question, "What do snowflakes do?" during a group time and brainstorm the possibilities. Have each child imagine that he is a snowflake and record his dictation on his page. Encourage the child to illustrate his story. Then bind the completed pages together to make a class book. Share the stories during the next circle time, being sure to acknowledge the author-illustrator of each page.

If I were a snowflake...

I'd whirl right to the tip of my mom's nose!

by David

Sing a Song of Self-Esteem

Now that your youngsters know that being different makes them special, they have something to sing about! So teach this little ditty and sing up a snowstorm.

(sung to the tune of
"She'll Be Comin' Round the Mountain")

We all are very different, yes, we know.
Yes, we know!   *(shout)*
We all are very different, yes, we know.
Yes, we know!   *(shout)*
From our heads down to our toes—
Like the little flakes of snow—
We all are very different, yes, we know.
Yes, we know!   *(shout)*

Snowflake Pattern
Use with "A Special Sharing" on page 126 and "A Snowstorm of Successes" on page 127.

Snowflake Cards

Use with "Double the Pleasure, Double the Fun" on page 127.

If I were a snowflake...

by

_____

Note to the teacher: Use with "If You Were a Snowflake…" on page 128.

Winter Where You Are

Whether your winter is cold and snowy, wet and rainy, or warm and sunny, these cross-curricular ideas and activities will create the perfect learning climate in your classroom.

ideas contributed by Lucia Kemp Henry

It's Winter! What's Our Weather Like?

Thunderstorms or snowstorms? How about brainstorms? This circle-time activity has youngsters brainstorming words that describe winter in your neck of the woods. To begin, have your students close their eyes and imagine a typical winter day. Invite each child to share a descriptive weather word; then write his response on a sheet of chart paper. Review the completed chart with students before displaying it in your classroom. Refer to the chart again in "Sing a Weather Song" (below).

Our winter is...

rainy	gloomy
cloudy	chilly
cool	damp
wet	muddy
dark	stormy

Sing a Weather Song

Once students are familiar with your list of weather words (see "It's Winter! What's Our Weather Like?"), have them sing the song at the right, replacing the underlined words with words from the chart. If needed, replace the italicized phrase with another phrase that more accurately describes your winter weather—such as *raindrops pouring* or *sunlight shining.*

(sung to the tune of
"If You're Happy and You Know It")

When it's winter in our town, it is [cold].
When it's winter in our town, it is [cold].
When it's winter in our town, we see
snowflakes falling down.
When it's winter in our town, it is [cold].

Winter Wear for Winter Where?

Would you wear mittens during winter in San Diego? How about shorts on a typical Detroit winter day? Help your little ones sort out winter weather differences with this group flannel-board activity. In advance, obtain pictures of different types of climates, such as rainy, sunny, snowy, and mild. (Calendars are a good source.) Laminate the pictures and then glue a strip of felt to the back of each one. Next, duplicate the clothing patterns on pages 135 and 136. Color, cut out, and laminate the clothing; then glue a strip of felt to the back of each piece. Place the pictures and clothing on a flannelboard; then invite students to match the clothes with the appropriate climate. Discuss the differences in clothing for each climate; then have students determine which set is most like the clothing needed for winter weather in your area.

Wonderful Winter Wear!

Now that your youngsters have warmed up to the idea of different winter climates, heat up their reading skills with these individual booklets. To prepare, duplicate for each child pages 137–139 and the clothing patterns most appropriate for winter in your area. (See pages 135–136. Do not use the hats.) Cut apart the booklet pages; then provide each child with a set of pages and a page of clothing patterns. Have the child follow the directions below to complete her booklet. When the glue is dry, stack the pages in order and then staple them together along the left side.

Cover: Write your name where indicated; then embellish as desired with various craft items.
Page 1: Color the page; then glue sand to the bottom of the page.
Page 2: Draw raindrops on the page. Squeeze yellow glue on the raincoat and boots; then use your finger to spread the glue over the coat and boots. Cut an umbrella canopy from fabric (see sample) and glue it to the umbrella handle.
Page 3: Color the page; glue cotton ball pieces to the coat and the bottom of the page to resemble snow.
Page 4: Color and cut out the clothing patterns. Glue them onto the figure and then color the head to look like yourself.

133

Winter Weather Movements

Surfing, sledding, or splashing around in puddles? What do you like to do in winter? Get your youngsters in the mood for the season with this fun movement activity. Use the pictures from "Winter Wear for Winter Where?" on page 133 and review the different types of winter climates. Tape each picture to a large sheet of paper; then have students brainstorm different outdoor activities appropriate for each climate. Write their responses on the paper. After the brainstorming session, have students recall which picture is most like the winter climate in your area. Then have them act out the activities listed for that climate. As an extension, invite a child to perform an activity from another climate and have the class guess what he is doing. Wow! Winter weather sure is fun!

sledding
building snowmen
throwing snowballs
ice skating

The Local Report

Watching winter weather is wonderful! Use the following suggestions to help give your youngsters a wide variety of weather-watching experiences.
- Take a field trip to the weather center at your local television station. Or invite a local weather reporter to come and speak to your class.
- If you have access to cable television in your classroom, watch and discuss The Weather Channel with your youngsters. If you do not have cable in your classroom, record a segment from The Weather Channel to view with your students.
- Have different students volunteer to watch the evening weather report and relay the report to the class the following day.

The Weather Center

Weather-Watching Center

The forecast for this dramatic-play area calls for fun, fun, fun! After all of the winter weather talk, your little ones will be eager to visit this weather-watching center and practice their forecasting skills. In preparation, make weather symbol cutouts and attach a strip of magnetic tape to the back of each one. Also make a weather center sign.

Place the sign in your designated weather center along with the weather symbols and a large map attached to a magnetic surface. (If a magnetic surface is not available, use Sticky-Tac adhesive on the symbols and laminate the map.) Have each little meteorologist observe the weather outside, predict the weather for the next few days, and then place the corresponding weather symbols on the map. Invite her to then use a pointer to give the winter weather report. There's sure to be a downpour of learning at this center!

Clothing Patterns

Use with "Winter Wear for Winter Where?" and "Wonderful Winter Wear!" on page 133.

Clothing Patterns

Use with "Winter Wear for Winter Where?" and "Wonderful Winter Wear!" on page 133.

Wonderful Winter Wear!

by _____

If winter in my town was hot,

I would wear my shorts a lot.

1

Booklet Pages 2 and 3

Use with "Wonderful Winter Wear!" on page 133.

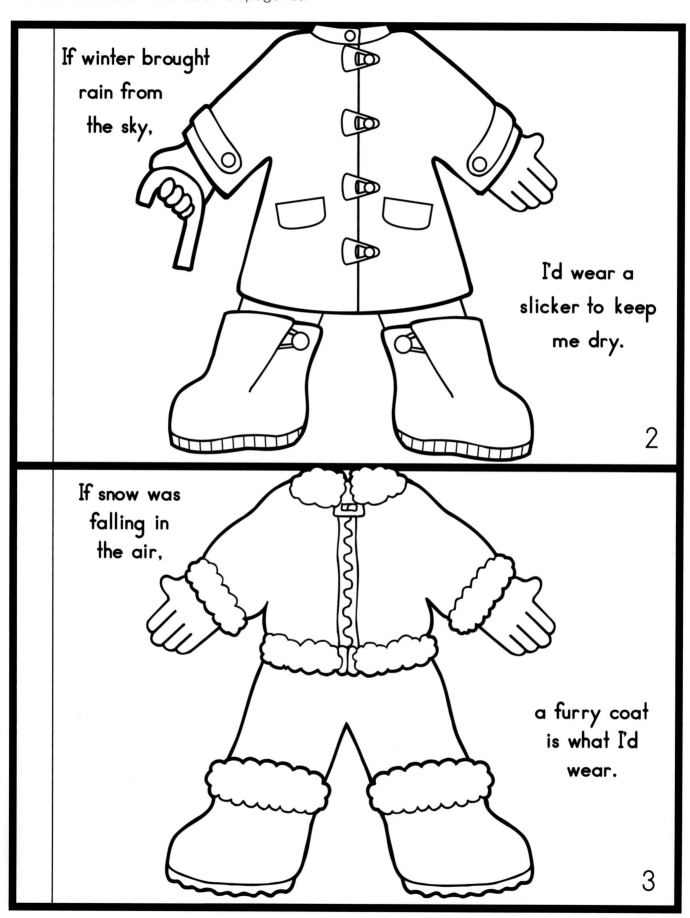

If winter brought rain from the sky,

I'd wear a slicker to keep me dry.

2

If snow was falling in the air,

a furry coat is what I'd wear.

3

Winter there.
Winter here.

This is my own
winter gear.

4

Ah, the fun and excitement of getting a letter! This unit is stuffed with postal-themed ideas that reinforce beginning sounds. So read on and get ready to SWAK (share with a kindergartner)!

ideas by dayle timmons

First-Class Phonics

And the Letter Says?

Introduce your phonics unit with this adaptation of the One Potato, Two Potato game. Program each of 26 index cards with a different letter of the alphabet; put each letter card into a separate envelope. Have your students sit in a circle. Give a child one of the envelopes, and instruct the class to pass it around as they chant the rhyme on the right. Invite the child who is holding the envelope at the end of the chant to open it. Ask, "Whom is your letter from?" Have the child respond, "It's from the letter [*D*]." Then reply, "What does [*D*] have to say?" Encourage the child to make the sound of the letter [*D*]. If the child needs help, have a few students name objects that start with [*D*]. After the letter is named and the sound is made, put another letter into circulation and start chanting again.

One letter, two letters,
Three letters, four,
Five letters, six letters,
Seven letters, more!

D says /d/, /d/, /d/.

Mail Song

Here's a quick song that's great for transitions. Use the letter cards made in "And the Letter Says?" Show one card at a time and sing the verse accordingly.

(sung to the tune of "B-I-N-G-O")

There was a letter on my mail
And [*b*] was its name-o.
[/b/, /b/, /b/, /b/, /b/]
[/b/, /b/, /b/, /b/, /b/]
[/b/, /b/, /b/, /b/, /b/]
And [*b*] was its name-o.

adapted from an idea by Randi Austin—Gr. K, Lebanon, MO

Matching the Mail

Stuffing these envelopes makes practicing initial consonant sounds a priority! To prepare, duplicate the alphabet pictures on page 143 or gather an assortment of stickers to represent the initial sounds. Put each picture in the upper right corner of a different envelope to serve as the stamp. Label an index card for each letter sound that is represented on the envelopes. Mix up the cards and envelopes and store them in a used priority mailing box.

To complete the activity, a student empties the box and sorts the envelopes from the cards. Then he inserts each card into its correct envelope, matching the letter to its beginning sound picture stamp. Once all of the envelopes are stuffed, have the child deliver them to you or an adult helper for checking. Reward efforts with a sticker or stamp of approval!

Listen Closely!

Mail matters more when your *own* name is on the envelope! This listening game is perfect for small groups. In advance, write each child's name on the front of a different envelope. (Include last names too, if your students are ready.) Laminate the envelopes or cover the front of each one with clear Con-Tact covering. Give each child her envelope and a dry-erase marker.

Call out words that have easily distinguishable beginning sounds. Instruct youngsters to listen to each word and identify the sound. Then have each child search her name for the identified letter and cross it out if it's there. When all the letters in everyone's name are crossed out, have children wipe off their envelopes for another round of play.

Mysterious Mail

Whose letter is this? Challenge your little ones to crack the code to these pictograms and receive special deliveries. Use copies of the alphabet pictures (page 143), picture stickers, or stampers to program each of a class set of business-size envelopes with a different student's name. Each letter should have a picture that represents the sound that letter makes (see illustration). Insert a special treat, such as a stick of gum or a bookmark, into the envelope before sealing it.

During a group time, explain to your little ones that you received a whole bunch of mail but need their help in figuring out whom to give it to. Show one of the envelopes. Have a volunteer call out the name of the first picture and then ask another volunteer to name the beginning letter. Write the letter below the picture. Continue in this manner with the rest of the pictures. Can students recognize the name? Have the recipient claim her special delivery!

Packed With Personality

This alliterative class book links phonics with a lot of creativity! To begin, have students imagine that they are packing a box to mail to someone. Explain that each child is to pack something that starts with the same sound as the beginning of his name. Encourage the child to name an item that he could pack. For more phonics practice, ask classmates to give the child some other choices. Direct each child to pick one of the items named. Then have students brainstorm some descriptive words that begin with the same sound as the child's chosen object.

Direct the child to illustrate his object to fit the description; then label his paper similar to the one shown. Bind students' pages between book covers cut from a grocery bag and then title the front cover as shown. If desired, decorate the cover with canceled stamps and twine. Read the finished book aloud, then give each child an opportunity to take the book home overnight to share with his family.

From:
Mrs. Timmons's Class

To:
Our friends and families

PRIORITY

RUSH!

Handle with care!

Danny put in delicious doughnuts.

Jasmine put in jazzy jewelry.

Parcel Pickup

Invite parents to participate in all the postal fun with this idea. To prepare, wrap a shoebox and its lid separately in brown paper and twine to resemble a parcel. Make a class supply of the parent note on page 143. Put a note in the box and send it home with a different child each night. Parents are to help their child fill the box with objects that begin with the letter of her choice.

The next day, have the child bring the box to circle time. At that point, dramatically announce that [Cassidy] has a special delivery for the class. Invite the child to open the box and show one object at a time to the class. When all the contents are revealed, have your youngsters call out the letter that they represent. Display the box's contents on a tabletop with a sign that says "A special delivery from [Cassidy] and the letter [s]!" Encourage students to visit the table during center time and use their phonemic spelling to make a list of all the objects.

At the end of the day, send the child's objects home in a large resealable plastic bag. Then send the box home with another student. Hmm, what will tomorrow bring?

Handle with care!

RUSH!

PRIORITY

This End Up!

A Special Delivery
from
Cassidy
and the
letter S !

Dear Parent,

We need a care package from you! We've been practicing our beginning sounds through postal-related activities. It is your child's turn to bring us a special delivery from a letter of the alphabet. Encourage your child to choose a favorite letter. Then look around your house for objects that begin with the sound of that letter. Include as many of the objects as you can in the box provided. Send this special parcel back to school tomorrow. We'll have a great time discovering which letter sent us such a cool collection of items.

Thank you for your involvement!

P. S. The items will be returned to you tomorrow!

Rainbow Dragon

Rainbow Dragon is coming to your classroom with this first-class collection of colorful learning fun!

ideas contributed by Lori Kent

Kimberly
Richard

Rainbow Tail

What's that dragon waggin'? His colorful tail, of course! Youngsters will explore six (or more!) colors when they make this creative dragon booklet.

To prepare:

Photocopy the dragon body and tail patterns (pages 148–149) on construction paper. Then, for each child, cut 4" x 5" pages from red, orange, yellow, green, blue, and purple construction paper. (Add additional pages of color if desired.)

To make the booklet:

Color and cut out the dragon body and tail. Then work with one colored page at a time. (This works well as a center activity spread over several days.) Write/copy/dictate the appropriate color word on the bottom of the page. Then cut out magazine pictures of that color and glue them to the page. When each page contains a collage of color, tape the pages together as shown, leaving just a slight space between pages. Then glue the attached pages to the dragon body where indicated. To close the booklet, accordion-fold the inside pages.

Invite small groups of children to read their books aloud to you. Then display each booklet (extended) on a board titled "Rainbow Dragons."

Rainbow Dragon's Wagon

With Rainbow Dragon as the host, show-and-tell has never been so colorful! In advance, enlarge and duplicate the dragon pattern (page 150) onto white construction paper. Then color, cut out, and laminate the dragon body. To make a wagon, cover the edges of a shallow box with the desired color of construction paper. Add cardboard wheels, a laminated construction paper handle, and a color word card to the wagon. Then post Rainbow Dragon near the wagon.

Each week, encourage children to bring correspondingly colored show-and-tell items to display in Rainbow Dragon's wagon. During group time, invite each child to tell about his item. Then change the color of the wagon and repeat the process. After you've featured all the colors, cover the wagon with a variety of colors and announce that week as rainbow week. (If desired, give a guideline, such as "Each show-and-tell item must have at least three different colors in order to be displayed in Rainbow Dragon's wagon.")

Rainbow's Sing-Along Song

This little ditty will capture your kinesthetic kids right from the start—and all listening ears will be fine-tuned to catch their cues! In advance, photocopy the dragon pattern (page 150). Color the dragon's front with rainbow colors and add other details as desired. Cut out and laminate the pattern; then glue a large craft stick to the back to make a stick puppet. Next, copy the song to the right on chart paper. (If desired, use the corresponding color for each color word.) Then cut a class supply of crepe paper streamers in the colors mentioned in the song. When you're ready to sing this song, distribute the streamers among your students. Instruct each child to wave his streamer in a wide rainbow arch when he hears that color in the song. Once children are familiar with the song, invite them to exchange streamers and sing the song again using their new colors. It's really quite a sight!

Rainbow's Song
(adapted to the tune of "I'm a Little Teapot")

My name is Rainbow Dragon,
And I live by the sea.
I love to play with colors.
Won't you come play with me?
When you hear a color,
Wave that color high.
And I will see your rainbow
As I fly through the sky!

Yellow, red, and purple
In the sky so bright.
Green, blue, and orange
Flying with delight.
Orange, blue, and yellow
Every now and then.
Green, red, and purple
Coming back again.

Fit for a Dragon!

Your children will construct all sorts of color concepts when they design a home that's fit for Rainbow Dragon! To prepare, stock your block center with a supply of colorful scarves, sheer gauzy fabric, and crepe paper streamers. When children visit this center, encourage them to use the supplies to design a home for Rainbow Dragon. If desired, invite children to use art supplies to make dragons to house in the delightful dragon homes!

Rainbow Drops

Scoop up a bunch of color practice with this activity that also reinforces fine-motor skills. To prepare, fill a large bowl with assorted colors and sizes of pom-poms. Arrange the large bowl in a center along with an ice-cream scoop, a pair of tongs and/or chopsticks, and paper bowls. To do this activity, have a child use the ice-cream scoop to scoop a bunch of pom-poms into a paper bowl. Then encourage the child to use the tongs or chopsticks to separate the scoop of pom-poms into different color groups. When his work has been checked, have the child return the rainbow drops to the large bowl and mix them up to prepare for the next center visitor.

adapted from an idea by Elaine Sheerin
New Bedford, MA

Beyond the Rainbow!

Fly above and beyond the colors of the rainbow with this classification activity. To prepare, place a box of 64 or more assorted crayons in a center along with a supply of white 6" x 6" construction paper squares. When a child (or small group of children) visits this center, encourage her (or them) to sort the crayons into groups of colors that are similar—or in the same family. Have each child select which color group she'd like to work with and then color one white square using all the colors in that color group. Next, help each child mount her work on a larger square of a dark color of construction paper. Mount each child's work on a board titled "Beyond the Rainbow!"

Note: *The Crayola Counting Book* by Rozanne Lanczak Williams provides a complementary literature extension for this activity.

adapted from an idea by Maureen Tiedemann—Gr. K
Holy Child School, Hicksville, NY

Dragon Puffs

Any dragon would be proud to puff out these fluffy treats! To make one, use different colors and combinations of food coloring to color several different bowls of water. Then cut two marshmallows in half. Color three of the marshmallow halves by using toothpicks to dip the marshmallows in the colored water. (The fourth half is yours for snacking!) Next, arrange the three colored marshmallow halves on a graham cracker square. Microwave the graham cracker–marshmallow combination for five to eight seconds. When they're cool, these dragon puffs make a colorful tasty treat!

The Magic School Bus: Liz Makes a Rainbow
Written by Tracey West
Illustrated by Jim Durk

From the animated TV series based on The Magic School Bus books comes this colorful tale featuring an active little dragon named Liz. Two hardworking children are stumped when they attempt to paint a rainbow with only four different colors of paint. But leave it to Liz to show the way to save the day! Extend this story with the activity described in "Rainbow Stew" on page 147.

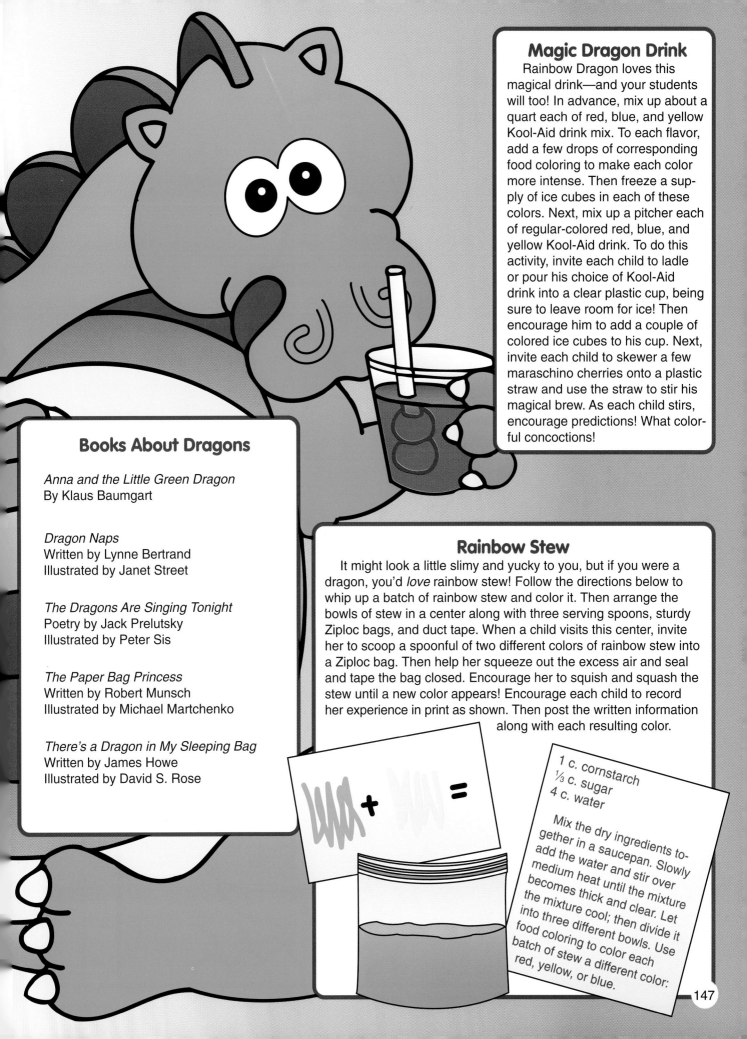

Magic Dragon Drink

Rainbow Dragon loves this magical drink—and your students will too! In advance, mix up about a quart each of red, blue, and yellow Kool-Aid drink mix. To each flavor, add a few drops of corresponding food coloring to make each color more intense. Then freeze a supply of ice cubes in each of these colors. Next, mix up a pitcher each of regular-colored red, blue, and yellow Kool-Aid drink. To do this activity, invite each child to ladle or pour his choice of Kool-Aid drink into a clear plastic cup, being sure to leave room for ice! Then encourage him to add a couple of colored ice cubes to his cup. Next, invite each child to skewer a few maraschino cherries onto a plastic straw and use the straw to stir his magical brew. As each child stirs, encourage predictions! What colorful concoctions!

Books About Dragons

Anna and the Little Green Dragon
By Klaus Baumgart

Dragon Naps
Written by Lynne Bertrand
Illustrated by Janet Street

The Dragons Are Singing Tonight
Poetry by Jack Prelutsky
Illustrated by Peter Sis

The Paper Bag Princess
Written by Robert Munsch
Illustrated by Michael Martchenko

There's a Dragon in My Sleeping Bag
Written by James Howe
Illustrated by David S. Rose

Rainbow Stew

It might look a little slimy and yucky to you, but if you were a dragon, you'd *love* rainbow stew! Follow the directions below to whip up a batch of rainbow stew and color it. Then arrange the bowls of stew in a center along with three serving spoons, sturdy Ziploc bags, and duct tape. When a child visits this center, invite her to scoop a spoonful of two different colors of rainbow stew into a Ziploc bag. Then help her squeeze out the excess air and seal and tape the bag closed. Encourage her to squish and squash the stew until a new color appears! Encourage each child to record her experience in print as shown. Then post the written information along with each resulting color.

1 c. cornstarch
⅓ c. sugar
4 c. water

Mix the dry ingredients together in a saucepan. Slowly add the water and stir over medium heat until the mixture becomes thick and clear. Let the mixture cool; then divide it into three different bowls. Use food coloring to color each batch of stew a different color: red, yellow, or blue.

Dragon Body Pattern
Use with "Rainbow Tail" on page 144.

Glue here.

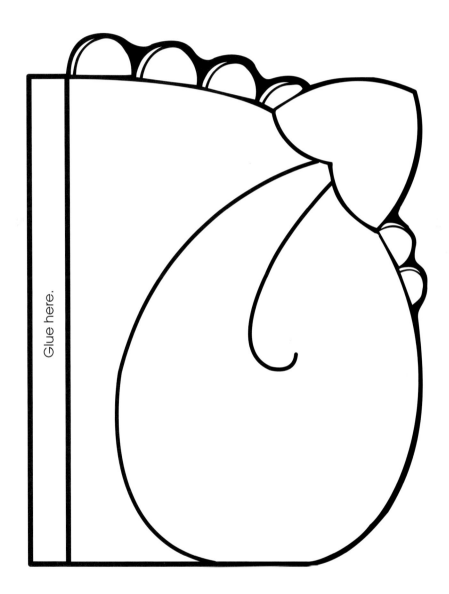

Glue here.

Dragon Pattern
Use with "Rainbow Dragon's Wagon" on page 144
and "Rainbow's Sing-Along Song" on page 145.

From Hives to Honey

Buzz, buzz, buzz! Spring is in the air and so are the bees! Get your whole hive humming with these cross-curricular ideas and activities that are as sweet as honey!

ideas contributed by kindergarten teachers

Mmmmmm! Honey!

What's the best thing about bees? Why, it's honey, honey! Buzz into your bee unit with this sweet study of the five senses. To prepare, program a chart similar to the one shown. Provide each child with a cup containing a small amount of honey. Invite your little bees to use their five senses to examine the honey, but do not tell them what it is. After a few minutes of investigation, have youngsters describe the honey. Write their responses on the chart; then have them guess what the mysterious sweet substance is. If youngsters are still stumped, have them sharpen their sense of hearing as you quietly whisper, "Buzz, buzz, buzz."

Nancy Provenzano—Gr. K, Galloway Kindergarten Charter School
Smithville, NJ

5 Senses Study

Seeing — It's yellow.
Smelling — It smells sweet.
Touching — It's sticky!
Tasting — It tastes sweet!
Hearing — It doesn't make any noise.

Flight of the Bumblebee

Use this idea and watch gross-motor skills and class cooperation take flight. Have students stand in a circle and hold the edges of a parachute. Place a stuffed bee in the center of the parachute. Invite students to make the bee fly by shaking the parachute up and down. If desired, play Rimsky-Korsakov's "Flight of the Bumblebee" during the activity. For an added challenge, hold up a number card. Have students read the number and send the bee flying that many times. Goin' up!

Leslea Walker—Gr. K
Ridgeway Nursery School
White Plains, NY

151

What's All the Buzz About?

Place this display in a hallway and the entire school will soon be buzzing by. To prepare, mask the facial features on the large bee pattern (page 155); then make a class supply of bees. Have each child personalize, color, and cut out his bee. Then help him cut out a small circle in the bee's face as shown. Glue a photograph of the child behind the circle so that his face shows through the opening. Cut a large beehive from bulletin board paper. Then mount the bees and hive on a wall or bulletin board.

Explain the meaning of the saying, "What's all the buzz about?" Then have each student dictate (or write) something new and exciting that is happening at home or at school. Mount his response beside his bee. If desired, frequently change the students' captions on the display as needed. What's all the buzz about? This unique display!

adapted from ideas by Judi Lesnansky—Title I K–4, New Hope Academy, Youngstown, OH
Robin Jolley—Gr. K, Janie Howard Wilson Elementary, Lake Wales, FL

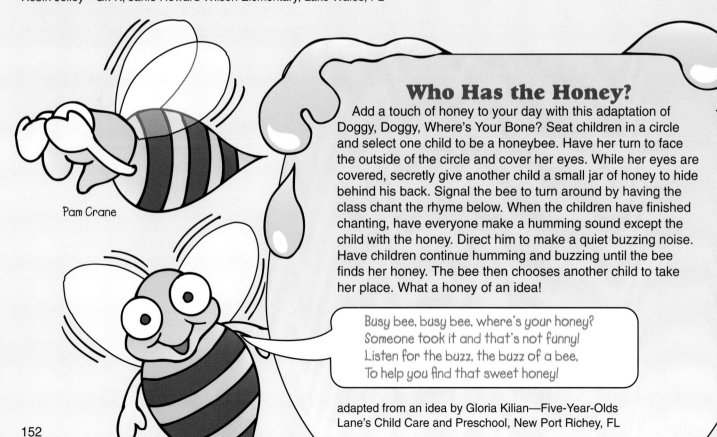

Pam Crane

Who Has the Honey?

Add a touch of honey to your day with this adaptation of Doggy, Doggy, Where's Your Bone? Seat children in a circle and select one child to be a honeybee. Have her turn to face the outside of the circle and cover her eyes. While her eyes are covered, secretly give another child a small jar of honey to hide behind his back. Signal the bee to turn around by having the class chant the rhyme below. When the children have finished chanting, have everyone make a humming sound except the child with the honey. Direct him to make a quiet buzzing noise. Have children continue humming and buzzing until the bee finds her honey. The bee then chooses another child to take her place. What a honey of an idea!

Busy bee, busy bee, where's your honey?
Someone took it and that's not funny!
Listen for the buzz, the buzz of a bee,
To help you find that sweet honey!

adapted from an idea by Gloria Kilian—Five-Year-Olds
Lane's Child Care and Preschool, New Port Richey, FL

152

A+ Behavior

This positive management idea will bring out the best in your little bees. To prepare, mask the stripes on the large bee pattern (page 155); then duplicate a bee for each child. Label the wing of each bee with a different child's name. Cut out and laminate the bees. Then mount them on a wall or bulletin board. If desired, decorate an inexpensive clay pot or plastic container to resemble a honey pot. Then fill the pot with treats.

Review with your class examples of positive "bee-havior," such as walking quietly in the hallway or helping one another. When a little one demonstrates good behavior, use a dry-erase marker to draw a stripe on his bee. When a child has earned a predetermined number of stripes, offer him a treat from your honey pot. Use a tissue to wipe the stripes from his bee and "bee-gin" again!

Jan Freshwater—Gr. K, Lake Norman Elementary
Mooresville, NC

A+ "Bee-havior"!

Tim
Angel
Aziz
Tony
Karla
Deanne
Stephen
Cara
Mika
Keesha

P Is for Pollinate!

This small-group activity will have youngsters buzzing over letter recognition and sound association. To prepare, duplicate the hive pattern on page 157. Color, cut out, and laminate the hive. Then tape it to a plastic bowl. Next, make several construction paper copies of the flower pattern on page 155. Tape each flower to the floor near the hive. Then place a piece of Alpha-Bits cereal on each flower.

Explain to a small group of children that bees collect pollen from flowers and bring it back to the hive to eat. Invite each child, in turn, to act like a bee and then "fly" to a flower. Have her pick up the pollen (cereal), identify the letter, and then bring it back to the hive. If student ability allows, have the child make the letter sound as she flies back to the hive. When all of the pollen has been collected and placed in the hive, reward each of your bees with a handful of fresh Alpha-Bits cereal. Mmmm, this pollen sure is tasty!

Judi Lesnansky—Title I K–4, New Hope Academy, Youngstown, OH

Pick a Peck of Pollen

If youngsters enjoyed the activity in "P Is for Pollinate!" try this variation in your math center. To prepare, make a supply of construction paper flowers from the pattern on page 155. (Or use the flowers from "P Is for Pollinate!") If desired, laminate each flower for durability. Place the flowers on a table and then place pollen (bingo chips) in the center of each flower.

To play the game, the first player rolls a die, reads the number, and then collects that many pieces of pollen from the flowers. The game continues in this manner until all of the pollen has been collected. My, what hard-working bees!

Roberta M. Neff, Espy Elementary, Kenton, OH

"Marble-ous" Bees!

Grab a pan and get your marbles! It's time to make some bees! To make one bee, cut yellow construction paper into the shape of a bee's body. Place the bee shape in a small pan. Next dip a few marbles in black paint and then drop them into the pan. Gently tilt the pan to roll the marbles over the bee, covering it with black stripes. Remove the marbles and set the bee aside to dry. Cut a coffee filter into four sections as shown. Then glue one of the sections onto the bee for a wing. Bend a black pipe cleaner and tape it to the back of the bee's head as shown. Finally, add a black pom-pom nose and a black dot for an eye. Bzzz! Bzzz! Bzzz!

Inez Hughes—Gr. K, FL Moffett, Center, TX

Give Me a B!

Youngsters will swarm to this center that focuses on the letter *B*. To prepare, make an enlarged copy of the hive on page 157 on tan tagboard. Program the hive as shown. Then laminate it and cut it out. Next, have youngsters search through magazines and cut out small pictures of objects that begin with the letter *B*. Then have them cut out a variety of other pictures. Set the pictures aside. Next, make a supply of construction paper bees from the patterns on page 156. Cut out each bee and glue a magazine picture to its wing. Color and laminate the bees. Then place them in a center along with the hive.

Invite each student to find the bees with *b* pictures and then place them on the "*B*-hive." If desired, make additional hives for each letter represented in the pictures—such as an "*A*-hive" or a "*C*-hive." Then have the student place each bee on its corresponding hive. Ahhh! Hive, sweet hive!

Jennifer Barton—Gr. K, Elizabeth Green School, Newington, CT

A "Bee-dazzling" Display!

This crafty display is the bee's knees! In advance, collect a supply of toilet paper tubes and paper towel tubes. Cut each tube into inch-long pieces. Glue the tubes' sides together to form a hive. Cover a bulletin board with yellow paper; then use pushpins to mount the hive on the board as shown. Next, provide each child with three segments of a foam egg carton. (Wash throughly before using.) Have her paint the cups yellow and black to resemble a bee. When the paint is dry, help her poke pipe cleaners through the cups for legs and antennae. Then have the child glue a pair of waxed paper wings to the bee. Finally, mount the bees around the hive.

Becky Barker—Gr. K
Discovery Days, First Baptist Church, Allen, TX

Large Bee Pattern

Use with "What's All the Buzz About?" on page 152 and "A+ Behavior" on page 153.

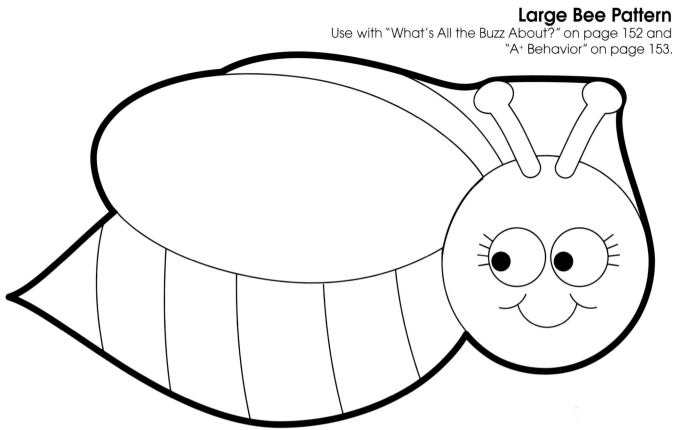

Flower Pattern

Use with "*P* is for Pollinate!" and "Pick a Peck of Pollen" on page 153.

Hive Pattern

Use with "*P* Is for Pollinate!" on page 153 and
"Give Me a *B!*" on page 154.

A Tribute to Trees

Use these tree-themed activities to capture the blossoming, budding wonderment of trees as your students honor National Arbor Day by creating this magnificent classroom display!

by Lucia Kemp Henry

Get the Feel for It

Challenge youngsters to feel their way through this tactile activity using their "tree-mendous" problem-solving skills! In advance, place a twig, leaf, walnut, pinecone, and piece of bark into separate brown paper bags. Gather your little investigators and tell them that each bag holds a clue to what they will be studying. Invite a volunteer to close her eyes and place her hand inside a bag. Ask her to describe the shape and texture of the object and then guess what it is. Then have her show the object to the class. Continue in this manner with the remaining bags. Display all five clues and then ask for students' conclusions about the topic of study, leading them to "trees" if necessary. Finish the activity by sharing *Crinkleroot's Guide to Knowing the Trees* by Jim Arnosky.

Hug a Tree Today!

Embark on this hands-on activity that gets your little woodworkers up close to a tree! First, give each pair of students two six-inch squares of white paper and a piece of brown crayon. Then take your class outside to mingle with the trees. Ask each child to close his eyes, touch the bark of a tree, and describe to his partner what it *feels* like. Next, ask each child to open his eyes and describe what the bark *looks* like. Then ask one child in each pair to hold a paper square flat on the tree while his partner uses the side of the crayon to create a rubbing. (If you do not have access to real trees, share books with photographs or drawings of tree trunks, and have each child create his own bark design.) Have partners change roles and repeat the crayon-rubbing activity. Ask your youngsters to glue their bark rubbings onto a length of brown bulletin board paper to create a large tree trunk. Later, staple the top edge of the tree trunk to a bulletin board so the bottom edge touches the floor. Then tape the lower section of the trunk to the wall. Complete this model tree with the four activities on page 159. What a great way to spruce up your classroom!

Getting to the Root of It!

Down, down, down go the roots and up, up, up grows a tree! Show your little ones a picture of tree roots from a reference book, such as *The Tree* by Gallimard Jeunesse and Pascale de Bourgoing. Ask them to describe what a tree's root system looks like and then point out where the thickest and thinnest roots are located. Discuss how the roots keep the tree from falling over when the wind blows and how they carry water to the tree's trunk and leaves. Then create a root system for your classroom tree. Give each of several children a length of brown crepe paper streamer to tape to the bottom of the tree trunk and onto the floor to represent the larger roots. Provide the remaining children with lengths of thick brown yarn to tape onto the streamers to represent the thinner roots. Remind students to watch where they step so they don't uproot their work!

"Leaf" It to Us!

Top off this terrific tree with student-made leaves! Collect real leaves for your youngsters to observe. Ask each child to carefully look at a leaf and describe its color and vein pattern. Explain that the leaves make food for the tree. Next, make a construction paper copy of the leaf pattern on page 161 for each child. Have small groups of students sponge-paint their leaves green and then use green-tinted glue to add veins. When the paint and glue are dry, have each child cut out her leaf. Then staple or tape your youngsters' fabulous foliage to the branches of the classroom tree.

Branching Out

Your budding tree experts will reach for the treetops as they create the branches for their tree model. Step outside with your class to observe the branches of a real tree. Explain that the branches give the tree its shape. Show examples of how the branches twist and turn. Return to the classroom and give each child a 1' x 2' strip of brown bulletin board paper. Demonstrate how to roll the paper into a tube, twist it into a branchlike form, and then tape it closed, as shown. Then help each child roll, twist, and tape his paper. Finally, arrange and staple (or tape) the branches above the trunk. Your classroom tree is shaping up!

Finishing Touches

If desired, label word cards with the parts of the tree (trunk, roots, branches, leaves) and add them to the display along with the title "Tree-mendous!" Later, encourage your tree experts to tell you about each part of the classroom tree. Then allow your youngsters to stretch out as they dramatize "I Am a Tree!" on page 160. Trees are top-notch!

leaves

Trees Are Our Friends

Plant some respect for trees with this thoughtful activity. In advance, cut two large tree shapes from bulletin board paper. Label one tree "A tree is…" and the other one "A tree has…" Post the trees near the model tree created in the activities on pages 158 and 159. Read aloud the book *Be a Friend to Trees* by Patricia Lauber. Show the book's illustrations as you ask each child to suggest a word to complete the phrase "A tree is…" Write each response on the matching tree. Next, use the tree parts from "Get the Feel for It" (page 158) to prompt responses to the phrase "A tree has…" Write youngsters' comments on the corresponding tree. What a forest full of facts your students have cultivated!

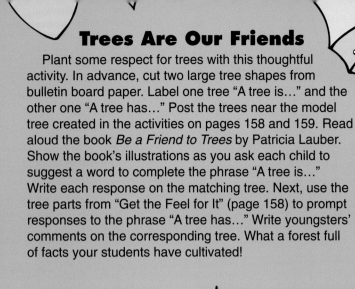

A tree is…
green
big
beautiful

A tree has…
leaves
branches
roots

Let's Tell About a Tree

Reinforce what your tree lovers have discovered about their woodsy friends with this song. Have your students sing the first verse several times, each time finishing the verse with a different word from the "A tree is…" tree (see "Trees Are Our Friends" on this page). Then ask them to sing the second verse in the same manner, using words from the "A tree has…" tree. There's so much to tell about trees!

(sung to the tune of "The Farmer in the Dell")

Let's tell about a tree.
Let's tell about a tree.
We know about a tree;
We know a tree *is* [green].

Let's tell about a tree.
Let's tell about a tree.
We know about a tree;
We know a tree *has* [leaves].

I Am a Tree!

When your youngsters perform this action rhyme, they will really get a feel for what it means to be a tree!

I am a tree. These are my roots.	*Stand tall and point to feet.*
They help hold me up	*Place feet apart, toes pointed out.*
Like a strong pair of boots!	*Rise up and lower on toes.*
I am a tree. My trunk is right here.	*Stand straight; put hands on hips.*
I'm dressed up in bark	*Pat legs and tummy with hands.*
In the front and the rear!	*Point to chest; point to back.*
I am a tree. My branches are wide.	*Stretch arms out to the side.*
They grow up and up	*Stretch arms overhead.*
And sway side to side!	*Wave arms side to side.*
I am a tree. These are my leaves.	*Wiggle fingers.*
They make cool, green shade	*Arch arms over floor in front of body.*
As they blow in the breeze.	*Wiggle fingers and sway side to side.*

Welcome to the Math-Review Zoo

A visit to this engaging zoo will create lots of math-skills practice. So come on. The fun is about to begin!

by Angela Van Beveren

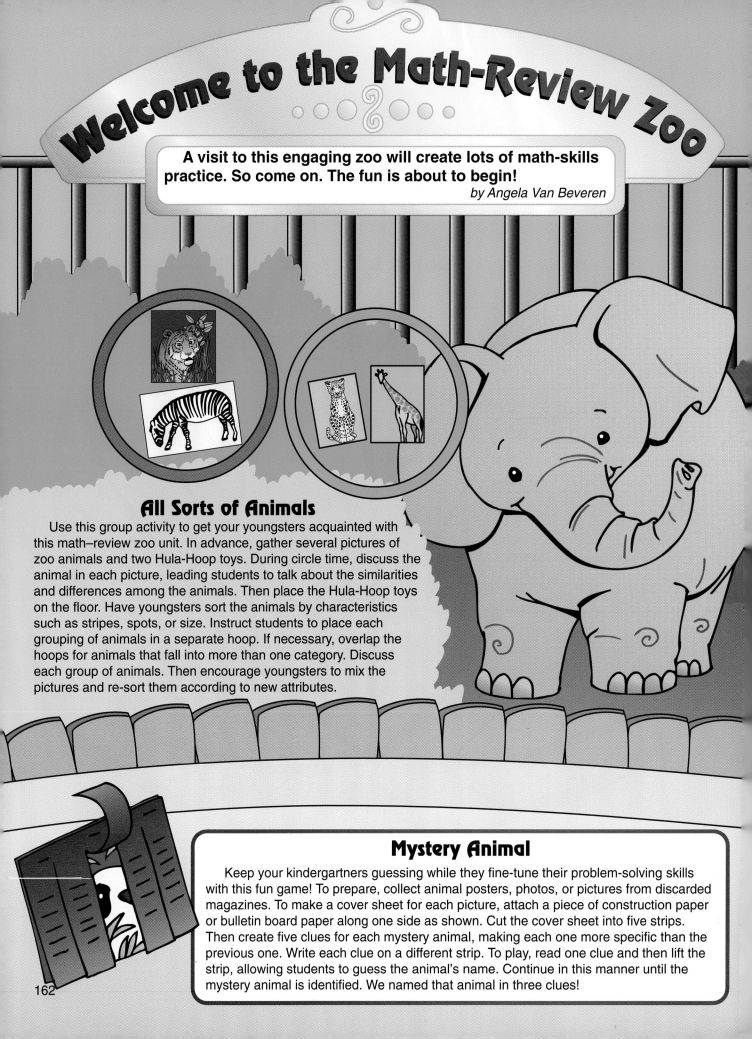

All Sorts of Animals

Use this group activity to get your youngsters acquainted with this math–review zoo unit. In advance, gather several pictures of zoo animals and two Hula-Hoop toys. During circle time, discuss the animal in each picture, leading students to talk about the similarities and differences among the animals. Then place the Hula-Hoop toys on the floor. Have youngsters sort the animals by characteristics such as stripes, spots, or size. Instruct students to place each grouping of animals in a separate hoop. If necessary, overlap the hoops for animals that fall into more than one category. Discuss each group of animals. Then encourage youngsters to mix the pictures and re-sort them according to new attributes.

Mystery Animal

Keep your kindergartners guessing while they fine-tune their problem-solving skills with this fun game! To prepare, collect animal posters, photos, or pictures from discarded magazines. To make a cover sheet for each picture, attach a piece of construction paper or bulletin board paper along one side as shown. Cut the cover sheet into five strips. Then create five clues for each mystery animal, making each one more specific than the previous one. Write each clue on a different strip. To play, read one clue and then lift the strip, allowing students to guess the animal's name. Continue in this manner until the mystery animal is identified. We named that animal in three clues!

How Do You Measure Up?

Here's an activity that really measures up! Explain to students that a baby giraffe can be six feet tall at birth. After a discussion, attach a six-foot length of adding machine tape to a wall. Then measure each child's height and cut a length of adding machine tape to match. Have the child label his length of tape with his name and height. After each child has been measured, have youngsters order the paper strips from shortest to tallest and then attach them to the wall next to the giraffe's strip. What an orderly activity!

Alexa 3 feet 1 inch

Matt 3 feet 2 inches

giraffe 6 feet

Zoo Snack

Don't feed the animals—feed your students instead! In advance, ask each of five parents to send in a snack item, such as cereal, mini marshmallows, crackers, pretzels, or chocolate chips. Arrange the snack items in bowls for easy student access. Give each child a 1" x 12" length of construction paper, a bingo marker, and a resealable plastic bag. Have her use the bingo marker to make ten dots along her strip of paper. Then instruct each youngster to use her strip to count ten of each snack item by placing one piece on each dot. After each dot has been covered, have her place the pieces in her bag and repeat the process with the remaining snacks. When you are ready for your little ones to eat, have them pour the snack mix onto a napkin and count the whole set…48, 49, 50!

Designer Zoo

Your youngsters will enjoy this fun activity, which combines patterning practice with an artistic flair for design! In advance, enlarge the animal patterns on page 166. Make enough copies of each animal so that each child in your class may choose one. Discuss with students the markings and patterns that various animals have, such as stripes on a tiger or spots on a giraffe. Next, have each child choose an animal pattern. Instruct him to use crayons or markers to create a new patterned coat for the animal he chose. Have him cut out his animal and glue it to the center of a 9" x 12" sheet of construction paper. Then display the finished products on a bulletin board titled "Designer Animal Duds!"

Zoo Stories

"Tell us more, please!" This is the phrase you'll hear when you play this addition and subtraction game with your little ones. To prepare, make a colorful copy of the cage pattern on page 167 for each child. Laminate the patterns for durability. Give each youngster a cage and a handful of animal crackers. Have each student manipulate his crackers to act out the number stories you say (for example, "Four animals were in a cage. The zookeeper took one out to give it a bath. How many animals were left?"). After getting the hang of this game, invite youngsters to make up and tell number stories while the rest of the class calculates the answer using the crackers. When all the stories have been told, allow students to snack on their animal crackers.

No Ordinary Lineup

It's time to get the animals in order! Use this activity to sharpen your students' listening skills. In advance, make several copies of page 168. Cut each sheet along the horizontal lines to create seven identical strips. Make one copy of the game mat on page 167 for each child plus one for yourself. Give each youngster a game mat and strip of animals. Have her cut the animals apart along the dashed lines. Place your own set of animals in a particular order on your mat; then give students oral directions for placing their animals in the correct positions. You might say, for example, "Zebra is third. Giraffe is last. Hippo is second. Gorilla is in front of Hippo. And Seal comes after Zebra." After all animals have been positioned, talk about the correct order and have students check their work.

Do Feed the Animals

Reward success with a tasty treat during this game, which has kindergartners counting and practicing one-to-one correspondence. To prepare, make a class set of the animal patterns on page 168. Give each child a copy of page 168 and a small cup of animal feed (cereal pieces). Provide each student pair or small group with a die. In turn, have each child roll the die, count the number of dots on the top surface, and then feed that number of animals by placing a cereal piece on top of each one. Play continues until each player has fed all her animals. When finished, invite youngsters to feed themselves a little snack!

Monkey Tails

No monkey business here! Ordering by length is a snap with this activity. In advance, copy page 169 to make a class set. Cut a two-foot length of brown yarn for each child. Distribute the copies and lengths of yarn. For each exercise, have each child cut three tails of different lengths and glue them to her paper in the appropriate order as shown. After completing the activity, have your little monkeys use tape to attach any leftover yarn to create their own tails. Then instruct them to order their tails from shortest to longest!

Animal Parade

This center activity allows your students to practice patterning and create a fashionable headband too! Place a supply of sentence strips, crayons, zoo animal stamps, and a stamp pad at a center. Have each youngster create a pattern with the stamps along his strip. Then invite him to color the animal prints. When his strip is finished, staple it to make a headband that fits his head. Have each youngster share his animal parade pattern with the class; then encourage him to wear his headband home. What fashionable animal apparel!

A Few in the Zoo

Kindergartners will love this clever partner game! Gather a supply of 20 or more plastic zoo animals, two cages (berry baskets or small boxes), and a die. (To make a die for this game, label three sides of a cube-shaped box with "M" for *more,* and three sides with "F" for *fewer.*) To play, each player selects a random number of animals and places them in his cage. In turn, each child rolls the die. If the die shows *M* on top, the player with more animals wins the round. If the die shows *F* on top, the player with fewer animals wins the round. If the players have chosen an equal number of animals, no one wins the round. The winner of each round takes all the animals from both cages, and her opponent selects a new set of animals from the reserve pile. Play continues until one player has collected all of the animals. It's fun to play A Few in the Zoo!

Animal Patterns
Use with "Designer Zoo" on page 163.

Cage Pattern
Use with "Zoo Stories" on page 164.

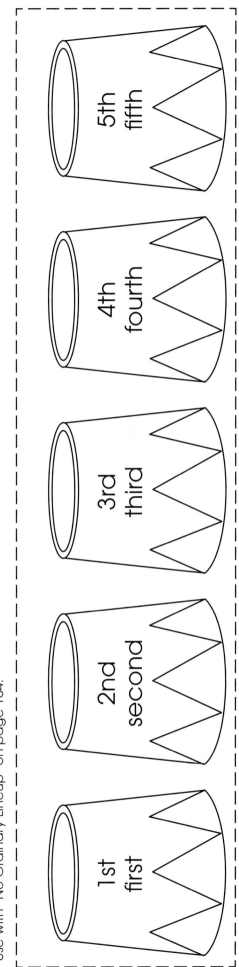

Game Mat
Use with "No Ordinary Lineup" on page 164.

5th
fifth

4th
fourth

3rd
third

2nd
second

1st
first

Animal Patterns

Use with "No Ordinary Lineup" and "Do Feed the Animals" on page 164.

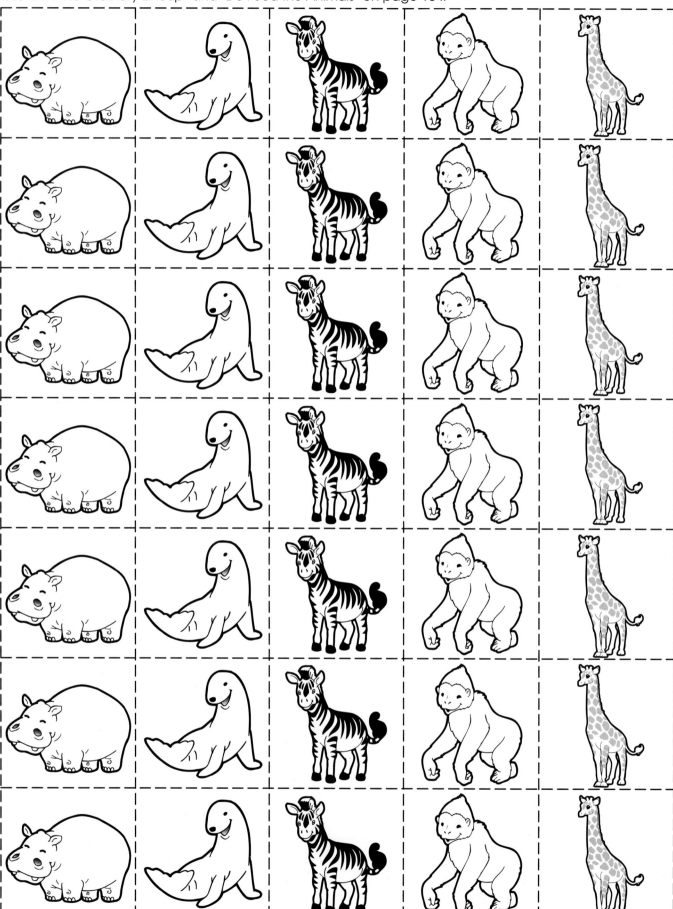

Monkey Tails

Cut a tail for each monkey.
Read.
Glue the tails in order.

These tails are in order from **shortest to longest.**

These tails are in order from **longest to shortest.**

Hooray for the USA!

It's time to start celebrating America! The 21 days from Flag Day (June 14) to Independence Day (July 4) have been declared by Congress as a period to honor our country. So use the following activities to help instill a little patriotic pride into young hearts and minds.

Salute Lady Liberty

Each of your students will be carrying a torch for the famous Lady Liberty when he creates this patriotic project! To begin, show students a photo of the Statue of Liberty from an encyclopedia or nonfiction book. Share several facts about the statue (see below) to familiarize youngsters with this famous American symbol. Then help each child follow the directions to make a torch of his own. It's a lot like Lady Liberty's!

Materials for one torch:

9" white paper plate paintbrush
¾ paper towel tube glue
green, white, and blue tempera paints masking tape
orange or yellow tissue paper scissors
pencil

Teacher preparation:

Mix the green, white, and blue paints to get a seafoam green color.

Directions:

1. Cut around the rim of the plate to form points.
2. Stand the paper towel tube on end in the center of the plate and use a pencil to trace around it. Then cut out the circle.
3. Fit the tube into the circle and secure it with strips of masking tape.
4. Paint the entire torch; then allow the paint to dry.
5. Cut three or four rectangles from the tissue paper. Gather the rectangles together and push one end of them into the top of the tube. Use glue to secure the paper.
6. Crumple and twist the remaining ends of the tissue paper to resemble flames.

Margaret Southard—Gr. K, Cleveland, NY

Statue of Liberty Facts

- Construction of the statue began in 1875. The statue was completed in France in 1884. Almost a year later, the statue arrived in New York Harbor.
- From the base to the torch, the statue is more than 151 feet tall.
- To give an idea of the statue's size, her nose is 4½ feet long and her index finger is eight feet long.
- To visit the Statue of Liberty, you have to travel by ferry to Ellis Island in New York Harbor.

With my hand on my heart,
That's how I start
The Pledge of Allegiance, you see.

I say I'll be true
To the red, white, and blue
And America, land of the free!

Ask me to recite the
Pledge of Allegiance for you!

The Pledge of Allegiance

Your students have probably been reciting the Pledge of Allegiance since the beginning of the year. But do they know what the words mean? Inform your youngsters that the Pledge of Allegiance is a promise to be loyal and true, both to our country's flag and to the USA itself. Demonstrate the proper way to stand when reciting the pledge—with the right hand over the heart. Snap an instant photo of each child standing this way, preferably with the classroom flag in the background. Copy a certificate from page 172 for each child. Have the child color her certificate and then attach her photo where indicated. Teach your students the poem on the certificate to remind them of the pledge's meaning. Then send the certificates home to stimulate some patriotic discussions!

Ada Goren, Winston-Salem, NC

Where's the White House?

What do you get when you take a popular party game, give it a patriotic twist, and sprinkle in some factual information? You get a game of Pin the White House on the Map! To prepare, duplicate the White House patterns on page 173 to make a class supply; then cut out the patterns. Attach a large map of the United States to a classroom wall. You'll also need a bandana (or another type of blindfold) and some Sticky-Tac adhesive.

Working with one small group at a time, gather around the map and give each child a White House cutout. Have the child write her name on the back of her cutout and then add a bit of Sticky-Tac adhesive. Explain that this game is similar to Pin the Tail on the Donkey, with the object being to stick the White House on the map as close to Washington, DC, as possible. Point out Washington's location on the map and then have the first player take her turn. During the game, share the interesting facts below. Your students will soon be experts on the executive mansion! Award a small prize to the child whose White House is closest to the nation's capital. Then give all your players a patriotic sticker for participating.

Ada Goren, Winston-Salem, NC

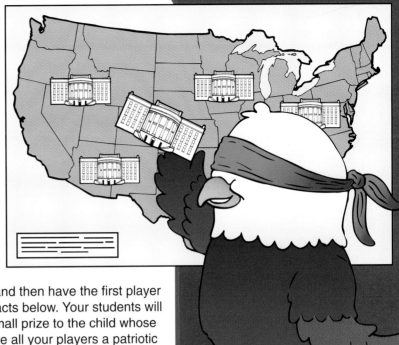

White House Facts
- Although George Washington oversaw the building of the White House, our second president, John Adams, was the first to live there.
- The Oval Office, located in the White House, is where the president works.
- The Red Room and the Green Room are rooms in the White House. They were named for the colors of their walls.

I'm proud to be an American because. . .

I can go to church anywhere.

Proud to Be an American!

Bring your mini unit to a star-spangled ending with this display! To prepare, make a class supply of the hat pattern (page 173) on white construction paper. Then, for each child, program the top of a sheet of 12" x 18" construction paper with "I'm proud to be an American because…" Encourage each youngster to decorate his hat using red and blue crayons, glitter, foil stars, and patriotic stickers. Then instruct him to cut out his hat and glue it below the programming on his sheet of construction paper as shown. Have him draw a full-body portrait of himself wearing the hat. Below the child's drawing, invite him to write (or dictate for you to write) an ending to the programmed sentence. Then display the finished projects on a bulletin board trimmed in red, white, and blue. Let's hear it for the USA!

Taryn Lynn Way—Gr. K, Los Molinos Elementary School
Los Molinos, CA

Certificates

Use with "The Pledge of Allegiance" on page 170.

With my hand on my heart,
That's how I start
The Pledge of Allegiance, you see.

I say I'll be true
To the red, white, and blue
And America, land of the free!

**Ask me to recite the
Pledge of Allegiance for you!**

With my hand on my heart,
That's how I start
The Pledge of Allegiance, you see.

I say I'll be true
To the red, white, and blue
And America, land of the free!

**Ask me to recite the
Pledge of Allegiance for you!**

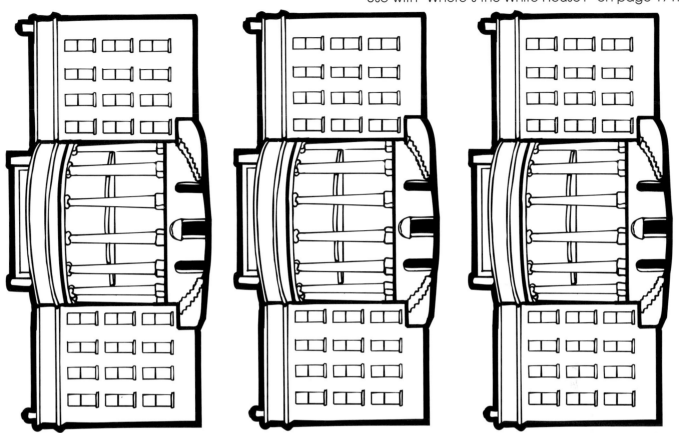

Hat Patterns
Use with "Proud to Be an American!" on page 171.

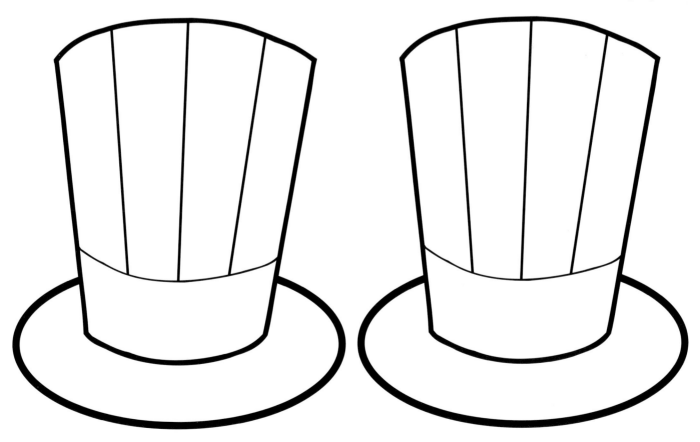

GIVE A CHEER FOR THE
END OF THE YEAR!

Looking for ways to keep you and your students motivated during those last few weeks of school? Look no further! These tips, ideas, and activities will keep you and your class on your toes until the very last day.

CLASS-MADE KEEPSAKES

Good behavior will abound with this management idea! Have weekly drawings for your class-made books and projects! During the last month of school, pass out good behavior tickets to students. Have each child write his name on his ticket and place it in a designated box or container. At the end of each week, draw one or two names from the container; then allow the winning students to choose a class book or project to take home and keep.

Kelly Mouw—Pre-K and Gr. K, McLeod Academy, Marion, IA

GRADUATION GOODY BAG

Bid a fond farewell to your youngsters with this idea— a goody bag full of fun and symbolism! To make one bag, duplicate the poem and note on page 176. Glue the poem to the outside of a paper lunch bag and then sign the bag. If desired, invite other teachers who have worked with the student to sign the bag. Next, place the note inside the bag along with the following items: a ruler, a handful of Hershey's Kisses, a pencil, a marker, a penny, and an eraser. On the last day of school, present each child with a bag and help her read the note inside. What a great way to say goodbye!

Mary Kibe—Gr. K, Visitation BVM, Norristown, PA

In this bag you will find some things

That hold the key to what your future brings.

It is with great sadness that I watch you depart

Because you have a special place in my heart.

Mrs. Roberts
Miss Ewing

SUMMER BIRTHDAY CELEBRATION

Little ones with summer birthdays will appreciate this idea! Designate one day during the last week of school for a summer birthday celebration. To prepare, ask parents of summer birthday children to send cupcakes, napkins, drinks, or other birthday goodies for the celebration. On the designated day, read birthday books, graph students' birthdays by month, make birthday cards and party hats, and play traditional party games. At the end of the day, sing "Happy Birthday" to each child with a summer birthday, and then serve a birthday party snack. Happy birthday to you!

Lin Attaya—Gr. K
Hodge Elementary, Denton, TX

STUDENT TEACHERS

This brilliant end-of-the-year idea has young-sters at the head of the class—teaching a lesson! To prepare for this activity, have each child begin thinking of his own talents and special interests. If necessary, help students brainstorm lesson ideas, such as blowing a bubble with gum, tying shoes, or preparing a special snack. Send home with each child a parent note explaining the activity and a copy of a simple lesson–planning sheet. When you have received a response from each child, create a schedule, and let the teaching begin! If desired, send parents a copy of the schedule and invite them to their little ones' lessons.

Lin Attaya—Gr. K
Hodge Elementary
Denton, TX

BANANA SPLIT BEHAVIOR

Encourage appropriate behavior with this cool dis-play. To prepare, cut out the parts of a banana split—such as an ice-cream dish, a banana, scoops of ice cream, hot fudge, whipped cream, and a cherry—from bulletin board paper. Next, program the ice-cream dish with a poem similar to the one shown and then mount it on a bulletin board or a wall. When your class dem-onstrates positive behavior, add a piece to the banana split display. When the final ingredient (a cherry) is added, treat your little ones to a banana split party. What a great way to go bananas!

Angelena Pritchard—Gr. K
Fountain Inn Elementary
Fountain Inn, SC

SUMMER'S HERE! LET'S SPLIT!

Let's build this banana split,
Piece by piece until it's done.
We'll earn each piece with good behavior.
Ice cream, whipped cream—oh, what fun!

BONUS BOOKS FOR GOOD BEHAVIOR

If you have acquired a large number of bonus points from book clubs, use them to order books as rewards for your students. During the last few weeks of school, present the books to students who demonstrate good behavior. Or hold a drawing on the last day of school for students who have earned a specified number of good behavior points. Good work, little ones!

Taryn Lynn Way—Gr. K
Los Molinos Elementary
Los Molinos, CA

Goody Bag Poem

Use with "Graduation Goody Bag" on page 174.

In this bag you
will find some things

That hold the key to
what your future brings.

It is with great sadness
that I watch you depart

Because you have
a special place in my heart.

©The Education Center, Inc. • *The Best of* The Mailbox® • *Kindergarten* • TEC60785

Goody Bag Note

Use with "Graduation Goody Bag" on page 174.

A 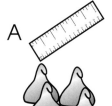 to remind you that there are always rules to follow

 to remind you that you are loved

A  to remind you that there are still many things to learn

A  to remind you to leave a good mark wherever you go

A  to remind you to use good sense

An  to remind you that it's all right to make mistakes

©The Education Center, Inc. • *The Best of* The Mailbox® • *Kindergarten* • TEC60785

Special Features

There's No Place

Ideas to Help Young Children Feel at Home in the Classroom

The first days of a new school year are often exciting for both teachers and students. But with that excitement, have you noticed that some youngsters arrive with a slight case of "the first-day jitters"? Choose from among this collection of ideas designed to ease those jitters by helping your little ones get to know you, each other, and their new school environment.

Before the Big Day

Oh, You'll Know!

Every parent who has dealt with the question "How will I know who my teacher is?" will be forever grateful to you for this idea! Choose a symbol from a classroom theme or a book that you plan to read on the first day. Then design something with that symbol that you can wear. For example, if you plan to read *The Cat in the Hat,* make a red-and-white striped hat from a paper plate and construction paper. (See additional suggestions below.) A couple of weeks before school starts, jot a quick note to each child telling her that you will be the teacher wearing for example, the tall, red-and-white striped hat. They'll know just what to look for!

- For a teddy bear theme, wear a headband with teddy bear ears.
- For a T-shirt theme, wear a very colorful, oversized T-shirt.

Deb Scala—Gr. K
Mt. Tabor Elementary School
Mt. Tabor, NJ

A Special Space

Foster a sense of classroom ownership and belonging by inviting each child to create his own special space in your classroom. A couple of weeks before school starts, mail each child a notecard inviting him (and his parent) to drop by your classroom on a designated date. (Use your open house date if your school holds one before classes start.) In the note, ask the child to bring requested school supplies with him on that day. When the child arrives, show him his cubby and where any larger supplies of his will be kept. Then give him a strip of tagboard labeled with his name. Encourage him to use an assortment of simple art supplies, such as stickers and stamps, to decorate his nametag. Then help him post his nametag on his cubby or at a table space. Youngsters will rest easy knowing they have a special space in their new kindergarten classroom. And you'll rest easy knowing all those sets of school supplies are organized before that hectic first day of school!

adapted from an idea by
Kiva English—Gr. K
Cato-Meridian Central School
Elbridge, NY

All About You!

You've all had those precious little ones who respond with shock when they learn that teachers actually *leave* the school building in the evenings and do ordinary things, such as shop in grocery stores, walk their dogs, or eat at restaurants. Create an all-about-you book to help your new batch of kindergartners get to know you and feel more comfortable in your classroom. In advance, gather a collection of photos that show you in settings or situations that children are likely to find interesting, such as with your family, friends, pets, or on a vacation. Arrange and mount the photos on sheets of construction paper. Then add simple captions for each picture. Laminate the pages; then bind them together behind a laminated cover. Display this book during meet-the-teacher times and the first few days of school. This book will be in high demand!

Angela Van Beveren
Alvin, TX

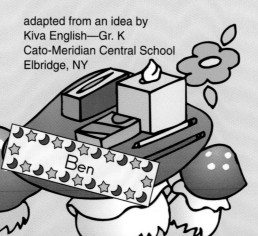

Like Kindergarten!

On the Big Day...and After

Mingling Manager

On that first day of school, do you have every intention to meet and greet each new child and parent with warmth and security only to be barraged by too many things happening at once? Here's a suggestion to ease that dilemma. Before students arrive, set up several play dough stations on your tables. If desired, offer written suggestions at each station to get the dough rolling—so to speak! When children and parents arrive, ask them to choose a place to work with the play dough. Because each parent and child is involved in this activity, you'll be able to meet and mingle at your leisure. You're also likely to find that this environment is a great one in which students and parents get to know each other as well. So let's get that dough rolling!

Leslye Davidson—Gr. K
Alameda, CA

Are We There Yet?

"Is it lunchtime yet?" "When can we go outside?" "Is it time to go home?" Sure, all of these are very important questions to a kindergarten child—but they also take up a lot of your time, don't they? This idea will help children understand the pace of each day as well as reinforce meaning and print. In advance, laminate a long strip of butcher paper. Glue a school cutout to the left side and a house cutout to the right side. Then use wipe-off markers to program significant times of your day along that strip. Next, add words, simple drawings, and/or pictures to depict your schedule for the first day of school. As you go through the first day, use reusable adhesive to post a cutout (such as a bus or other theme-related item) along the timeline. At the end of the day, program the timeline for the next day. As children become accustomed to this process, ask a child to move the cutout as the day progresses. "I can read just where we are!"

Angela Lavy Joel—Gr. K
Marlowe Elementary
Falling Waters, WV

The Magic Apples of My Eye

Let each child know how important he is to you with this "magic" idea that plants a seed of wonder. In advance, cut out a large tagboard apple for each child in your class. Using a craft blade, cut out a square from the center of each apple. (Judge the size of the apple and the cutout square by the size of your Polaroid pictures—described later.) If desired, add a stem and leaf to each apple. Then mount a large tree cutout on a classroom wall. On the first day of school, take each child's picture with a Polaroid camera. Invite each child to hold his picture by the edges and watch as the "magic" happens! When each photo has developed, glue it to the back of an apple and write the child's name on the front of the apple. Mount each apple on the tree and title the display "The Apples of [your name]'s Eye!" After explaining the meaning of the title to your students, watch them shine with pride!

Lou Monger—Gr. K
Glen Allen Elementary

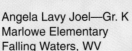

10:00 Library   12:00 Lunch   1:00 Centers

179

HAPPY BIRTHDAY TO YOU!

Make your little ones' birthdays extra special with these clever celebration ideas!

Birthday Flag

Let the rest of the school know when one of your students is celebrating a birthday. Purchase a birthday flag similar to the seasonal flags people use to decorate their homes. Mount a hanging bracket outside your classroom. Display the flag on days when a youngster is celebrating a birthday.

Casey Cooksey—Gr. K, Bruce Elementary School
Bruce, MS

Celebration Songs

Who says "Happy Birthday to You" should be the only song sung to celebrate a child's birthday? Create this special birthday cake to add some pizzazz to your song time. Make a birthday cake decoration and candles out of construction paper, glitter, and stickers. Then use a permanent marker to write the names of several favorite songs on the backs of different candles. Tape the candles to the cake. Have each birthday child "blow out" (choose) a candle and then have the class sing the song whose title is written on the back.

Paula Morris—Gr. K, Bells I. S. D., Bells, TX

Birthday Rap

Have your youngsters get in the rhythm of this birthday rap by starting off with a clap, clap, snap pattern! Instruct students to complete the pattern three or four times before reciting the rap. For each birthday, substitute the child's name in the second line.

We are friends, and we're here to say
It's [Connor's] birthday—hooray, hooray!
[He'll] have cake and ice cream too.
We hope [his] wishes will all come true!

Sharon Manley—Gr. K, Israel Putnam School, Meriden, CT

Special Thoughts

It's always nice to hear special things about yourself. Help your kindergartners feel extra special with a keepsake tape. Have students sit in a circle, with the birthday child sitting in the center. Label a cassette tape with the child's name and the date. Then encourage each child to think of a positive comment to say about the birthday child. Record student responses on the tape. You can even include the class singing a song or two or you reading a story—chosen by the birthday child, of course! Send the tape home with the featured child and encourage her to share it with her family. It will surely be one tape that is listened to over and over again!

adapted from ideas by
Kimberly Bush—Grs. PreK–K
Oakland Preschool and Kindergarten, Oakland, NJ

Ricke Bly—Gr. K, RTR Elementary, Ruthton, MN

The Birthday-Book Box

Decorate a plastic shoebox with birthday stickers and decorations; then fill it with a variety of birthday books. Invite the birthday child to select a book from the box to be read during your storytime. Every youngster will look forward to choosing a story on her special day!

The Berenstain Bears and Too Much Birthday by Stan and Jan Berenstain
Clifford's Birthday Party by Norman Bridwell
Arthur's Birthday by Marc Brown
Happy Birthday, Danny and the Dinosaur! by Syd Hoff
Happy Birthday, Thomas! by Rev. Wilbert V. Awdry

Stephanie Kneiding—Gr. K, Carpenter Y. R. Elementary, Orion, MI

Magic Moments

Got an extra few minutes before lunch? Did your students finish up before you had planned? Make the most of every moment by using these transitional activities. They're sure to fill each day with even more learning fun!

Mystery Student

This guessing game is based on the traditional song "Oh Where, Oh Where Has My Little Dog Gone?" In advance, write the verse below on a piece of chart paper and then laminate the chart. Whenever you have a few minutes to spare, use a wipe-off marker to program the verse to describe a particular student. Then sing the new verse, line by line, and encourage youngsters to echo it. Give volunteers an opportunity to guess the mystery student. Once her identity is revealed, wipe off the chart and begin again. Hmmm, I wonder who it could be.

Peggy Anderson—Gr. K
Theodore Roosevelt Elementary School
Pennsauken, NJ

Oh where, oh where has my little _____girl_____ gone?
Oh where, oh where can _____she_____ be?
With _____her_____ _____dress_____ so _____blue_____
And _____her_____ _____hair_____ so _____long_____.
Oh where, oh where can _____she_____ be?

It's Time to Tally

Here's a quick game to reinforce the math concept of tallying. Draw a score sheet similar to the one shown. Then pick up a marble or other small object, put your hands behind your back, and hide the marble in one of your hands. Bring your closed fists to the front and invite a student volunteer to guess which hand is holding the marble. If he is correct, have him make a tally mark on the corresponding side of the score sheet. If he guesses incorrectly, make a tally on your side of the sheet. Continue as time allows. Then have the group help you total up the tallies!

Harriet Velevis—Grs. PreK and K
Jewish Community Center Preschool
Dallas, TX

What's Your Number?

These number pendants will help not only with transitions but also with numeral recognition and sequence. Simply use a laminated number cutout and a length of yarn to make a different number necklace for each child. As youngsters enter your classroom each morning, give each of them a number. Then call out the numbers during transition times—such as coming over to group time, lining up, or washing hands—to better manage crowding. For younger students, you may want to call the numbers sequentially each time. But for more of a challenge, try directions such as "Odd numbers line up" or "Would the number that comes after eight please open the door?"

Bonnie Blanck—Gr. K
J. F. Dumont
Cincinnati, OH

hol-i-day

Clap, Clap, Clap Your Hands

Give phonemic awareness a hand with this quick activity. When you find yourself with a few extra unplanned minutes, grab a dictionary! Open it and call out a word. Encourage students to repeat the word and clap out the syllables. Continue with different words as time allows. Now this simple idea deserves a round of applause!

Karen Collins—Gr. K
Spout Springs Elementary
Flowery Branch, GA

One Potato, Two Potato

The next time your students are caught having to stand in line and wait a few minutes, try this fun game. Have each child make one big potato by clasping her hands together. Instruct youngsters to hold out their potatoes as you recite the traditional rhyme. Now here's the twist! Invite the owner of the potato you end the chant with to go to the front of the line. Continue countin' taters and changing leaders as time permits.

Caroline Henk—Gr. K
Rocky Branch Elementary
River Falls, WI

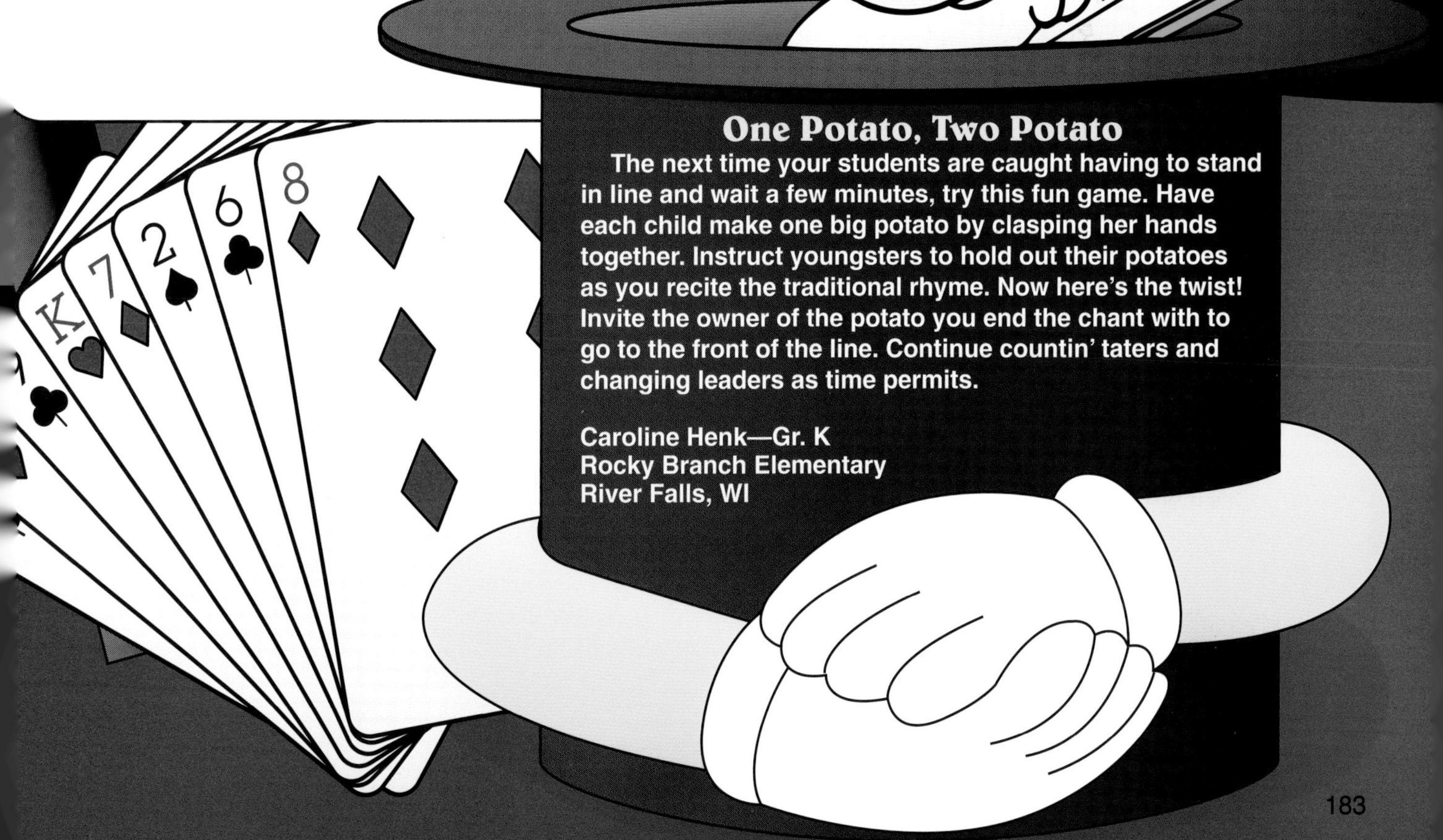

Jazzing Up Journals

Are you ready for some fresh and creative ways to keep your students excited about writing in their journals? We thought so! Here are some great ideas that were sent to us from teachers just like you!

Sniff, Sniff

Surprise youngsters with scented paper. Before school starts one morning, use a cotton ball to dab a colorless extract, such as peppermint or vanilla, onto a page in each child's journal. You're sure to get some sweet writing in return!

adapted from an idea by John M. Barrera
Las Americas Early Childhood Development Center
Houston, TX

Red-Letter Days

Show your youngsters a calendar that has the holidays printed in red. Explain that many people refer to special occasions as red-letter days. Then provide a special red pencil or pen for children to use to write in their journals on their birthdays or other very important days.

Linda Masternak Justice
Kansas City, MO

Who's That Special Kid I See?

Oh, it's me! Tape a piece of Mylar polyester film to a page in each child's journal. As the journals are passed out, tell students that they'll find someone special in there. When the proud giggles have subsided, have each child draw a self-portrait and write about how he looks. Mirror, mirror, on the wall…

John M. Barrera

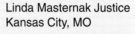

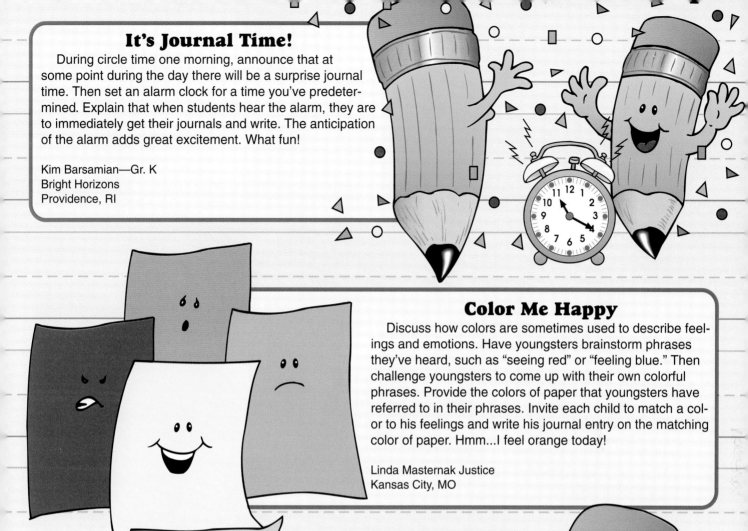

It's Journal Time!

During circle time one morning, announce that at some point during the day there will be a surprise journal time. Then set an alarm clock for a time you've predetermined. Explain that when students hear the alarm, they are to immediately get their journals and write. The anticipation of the alarm adds great excitement. What fun!

Kim Barsamian—Gr. K
Bright Horizons
Providence, RI

Color Me Happy

Discuss how colors are sometimes used to describe feelings and emotions. Have youngsters brainstorm phrases they've heard, such as "seeing red" or "feeling blue." Then challenge youngsters to come up with their own colorful phrases. Provide the colors of paper that youngsters have referred to in their phrases. Invite each child to match a color to his feelings and write his journal entry on the matching color of paper. Hmm...I feel orange today!

Linda Masternak Justice
Kansas City, MO

Juicy Writing

When children know that writing can bring treats, they become excited at journal time. Occasionally tape a stick of Juicy Fruit gum to each child's journal page and encourage her to fill her page with a juicy story.

adapted from an idea by John M. Barrera
Las Americas Early Childhood Development Center
Houston, TX

Journal Grab Bags

Remember the thrill of getting a grab bag and being surprised by its contents? Try these journal grab bags with your students. To make the bags, place various small items, such as fast-food toys or items found in your alphabet tubs, in paper lunch sacks. At journal time, invite each child to take a bag and write an imaginative story about the bag's contents.

Kathy Thurman—Gr. K
Southern Elementary
Somerset, KY

Nifty Nutrition

These ideas give your little ones food for thought and promote healthy eating habits!

Fabulous Foods

To get your youngsters thinking about good nutrition, have them complete this display. To prepare, make six large poster board cutouts, each representing a food in a different food group. Label each poster with the name of its group as shown. Then discuss with students the different types of foods they eat and in which group these foods belong. Next, provide each child with a discarded magazine, scissors, and glue. Have each youngster cut out pictures of foods and then glue them to the appropriate poster. Display the posters in a hallway to remind all students in your school about good nutrition.

Lisa Cohen—Gr. K
Laurel Plains Elementary
New City, NY

A Healthy Lunch

This healthy lunch idea is bound to create some conversation at home about proper eating habits! In advance, clean and dry a class set of empty milk cartons. Then make tagboard tracers that represent sandwich parts, such as a circle for meat, a wavy-edged circle for lettuce, a square for cheese, and a square trimmed to represent a slice of bread. On the day of the activity, give each child pieces of craft foam, appropriately sized to accommodate your tracers, in the following colors: one pink, one green, one orange, and two tan. Have each youngster trace the shapes onto the foam and then cut them out. Help her label each sandwich part with the corresponding food group's name. Have her stack the sandwich and then wrap it in a piece of aluminum foil. Give each child a paper lunch bag, a milk carton, and a small apple. Have her place her sandwich, carton, and apple in her bag. Discuss with students the components that make this lunch healthy. Finally, encourage each student to take her healthy lunch home, talk about it with her family, and then share her apple snack!

Cheri Miller, Claudia Lieding, and Mary Jo Sprunk—Gr. K
St. Charles Primary School
Chippewa Falls, WI

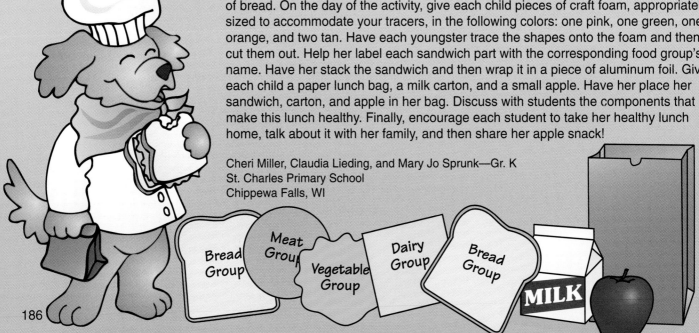

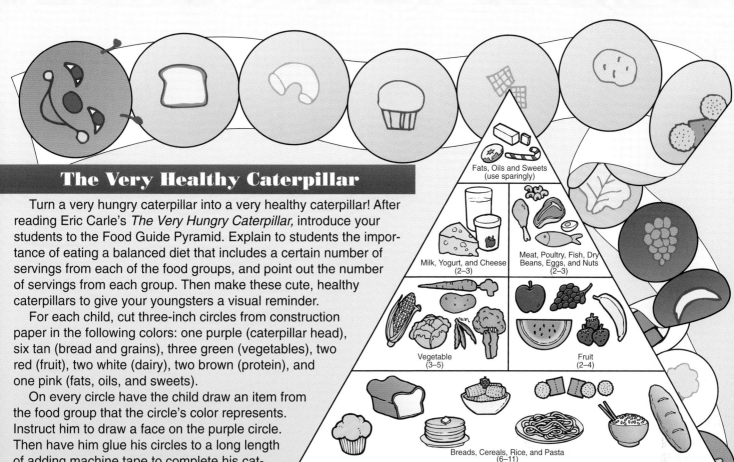

The Very Healthy Caterpillar

Turn a very hungry caterpillar into a very healthy caterpillar! After reading Eric Carle's *The Very Hungry Caterpillar,* introduce your students to the Food Guide Pyramid. Explain to students the importance of eating a balanced diet that includes a certain number of servings from each of the food groups, and point out the number of servings from each group. Then make these cute, healthy caterpillars to give your youngsters a visual reminder.

For each child, cut three-inch circles from construction paper in the following colors: one purple (caterpillar head), six tan (bread and grains), three green (vegetables), two red (fruit), two white (dairy), two brown (protein), and one pink (fats, oils, and sweets).

On every circle have the child draw an item from the food group that the circle's color represents. Instruct him to draw a face on the purple circle. Then have him glue his circles to a long length of adding machine tape to complete his caterpillar. Attach the caterpillars to a bulletin board titled "Very Healthy Caterpillars!"

Camille Maney—Gr. K
Alcoa Elementary School
Alcoa, TN

Chef Good Food

Your budding chefs will show you their knowledge of the Food Guide Pyramid with this project. In advance, cut a large triangle from white bulletin board paper for each child. Use a marker to create sections on each triangle as shown on the Food Guide Pyramid; then program each section with the correct food group. Cut a 24-inch length of red crepe paper (tie), two 3" x 18" white paper strips (arms), and a white paper chef's hat shape for each youngster.

Have each child color the back of a paper plate to resemble her face. Instruct her to glue the face to the top of her triangle and then glue a chef's hat to the head. Have each student cut food pictures from discarded magazines and glue them to the appropriate sections of her pyramid. Have her glue a pair of arms to the top portion of the triangle. Next, have each child tape a plastic spoon to the end of one strip and a plastic fork to the end of the other strip. Then help each youngster tie a length of red crepe paper below the paper plate. Label her chef's hat with her name. Attach the completed chefs to a wall and title the display "We're Cooking Up Some Good Eating Habits!"

Bernadette Hoyer—PreK
Coles and McGinn Schools
Scotch Plains, NJ

HELPING HANDS
MAKING THE MOST OF CLASSROOM JOBS

Do you have a classroom full of enthusiastic little hands that are raring to help out at a moment's notice? Choose from among the ideas in this unit to help you get the most out of classroom job opportunities.

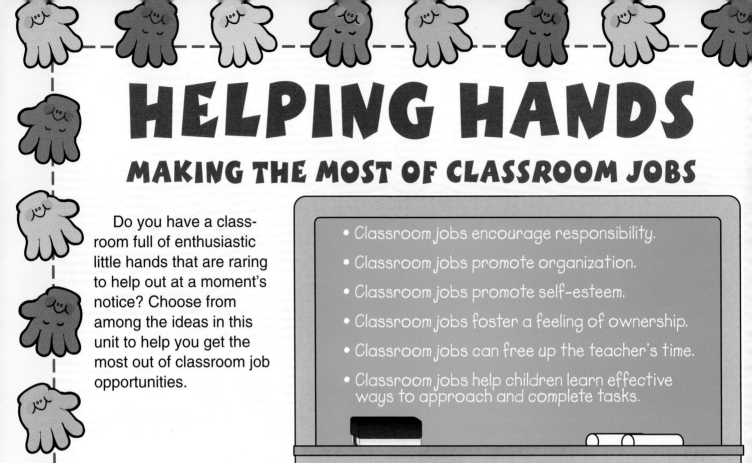

- Classroom jobs encourage responsibility.
- Classroom jobs promote organization.
- Classroom jobs promote self-esteem.
- Classroom jobs foster a feeling of ownership.
- Classroom jobs can free up the teacher's time.
- Classroom jobs help children learn effective ways to approach and complete tasks.

TWO BY TWO

When a task seems a bit overwhelming, teamwork is the ticket to get the job done! Assign selected classroom jobs to teams of two. For example, you might choose two people to accomplish a larger task such as cleaning up your block area. Ask the team members to work together to devise a plan to get the job done. Encourage them to support each other by complimenting one another's good work. Big jobs don't seem quite as big when you approach them two by two!

Julie Maffett
Child Care Association
Cocoa, FL

188

ANYBODY KNOW A GOOD PHOTOGRAPHER?

Sure, a whole lot of 'em! Instead of taking time out to be your own photographer, assign the job to your students. At the beginning of the year, use an old camera to teach children how to take photographs. Keep the camera in your dramatic-play area for practice. When you think students have the hang of it, create a press badge and a paper bag vest. Then, at each different event, assign a different child to wear the badge and vest and be the class photographer with a real disposable camera. Tell each child how many pictures she can take and then leave the rest up to artistic interpretation!

Ericka Way—Gr. K
Leslie Fox Keyser
 Elementary
Front Royal, VA

9 Ways to Clean Our Room

1. Clean up the floor.
2. Empty the trash.
3. Wipe off the tables.
4. Straighten the papers.
5. Push in the chairs.
6. Erase the board.
7. Put the crayons away.
8. Straighten the cubbies.
9. Wipe out the sink.

COUNTING ON HELP

Here's an idea for those days when the cleanup is a little too much for individual classroom helpers. Start by choosing a number, such as nine. Then ask the class to brainstorm *nine* ways to clean up the room. Write their responses on a chart. Have a different small group of children volunteer for each different idea listed. Then divide and conquer!

Michele Griffith—Gr. K,
Duffy Elementary,
West Hartford, CT

TABLE TOPPERS

If it's on a table, table toppers come to the rescue! Each week, assign a team of children to be table toppers. Then, when anything pops up that involves a table, you know just where your help is. Table toppers can set the table, clean messy tables, pass out supplies, etc. If it's on a table, they're tops!

AnnaLisa R. Damminger—Gr. K
Mullica Hill, NJ

PLAYGROUND PALS

Gathering up your playground equipment is made simple when you have playground pals. In advance, label a sheet of paper with the names of your playground toys and a simple drawing of each one (as shown). Laminate the page; then put it on a clipboard. When you're ready to go to the playground, have your chosen playground pal use a dry-erase marker to check off each item that is going out. When you come back inside, have that helper check each item in. If anything is missing, your playground pal can alert you right away and lead the search.

adapted from an idea by
AnnaLisa R. Damminger—Gr. K

STAFF MEETINGS

How important your little ones will feel when they get to attend staff meetings! If you assign classroom jobs by the week, hold a staff meeting midway through the week. After discussing areas of concern and praise, send your little workers off to complete their term of service with pride!

Vivi Sadel—Gr. K, Finletter School, Philadelphia, PA

Let's Celebrate!

Happy Hanukkah, Merry Christmas, and Happy Kwanzaa! No matter what holiday your youngsters celebrate, you'll find ideas in this unit to make each holiday special!

Handy Dreidels

This simple art activity will make an attractive bulletin board display and inspire your youngsters to spin, spin, spin a dreidel! To prepare, cut a 6" x 6" piece of white construction paper for each child. Pour a thin layer of blue tempera paint in a shallow pan. Help each child dip his hand into the paint and then make a print on his paper. Then have him dip his index finger into the paint and make a print at the base of his palm print as shown. After the paint has dried, use silver glitter paint to write the Hebrew letter *heh* on each print. Have each youngster cut out his dreidel print. Staple the dreidels to a bulletin board and then draw spinning-motion lines around each one. Title the display "Spin, Spin, Spin the Dreidel!"

Lisa Crystal—Gr. K, Bret Harte Elementary School, Burbank, CA

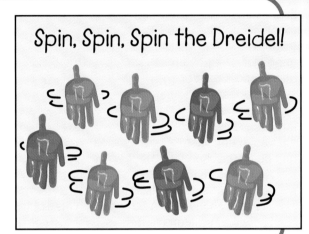

Spin, Spin, Spin the Dreidel!

Necktie Menorah

This flannelboard menorah will be just what you need to help celebrate Hanukkah! In advance, request donations of old neckties from parents and friends, or purchase them from a thrift store. To make a *menorah* for your flannel board, cut a sheet of gray felt as shown. To make the candles, cut the center 12 inches from each of eight neckties. Slide a strip of cardboard into each tie piece to give it shape. Use hot glue to close the ends and then glue a hook-side Velcro piece to the back of each candle so it will cling to your flannelboard. To make the *shammash* (the candle used for lighting the other candles), cut 15 inches from the center of a tie and then finish it as you did the other eight candles. Cut nine flames out of red felt. On each day, pretend to light a candle with the *shammash* by placing a flame atop one of the candles. Happy Hanukkah!

Janice McCarthy—Gr. K, Bicycle Path PreK–K Center, Selden, NY

A Dreidel Snack

This sweet treat will make your youngsters spin! Provide each child with a paper plate, a large marshmallow, a Hershey's Kisses candy, a pretzel stick, and access to blue-tinted vanilla frosting that has been heated slightly to thin it. Have each child push her pretzel into one end of her marshmallow. Then instruct her to hold the pretzel stick handle and dip her marshmallow in frosting. Have her unwrap her Hershey's Kisses candy and place its flat side on the bottom of the marshmallow. Invite her to spin her *dreidel* into her mouth!

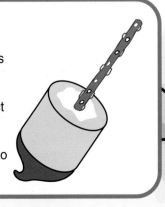

190

Christmas Tree Costume

This festive tree costume is sure to be a hit at your holiday program! Gather the supplies listed below and then follow the directions to make these simple costumes. Oh Christmas tree!

Materials needed for one costume:

white poster board
green tempera paint
red tempera paint
blue tempera paint
yellow tempera paint
triangular sponge

circular sponge
tinsel
glue
heavy tape
hole puncher
yarn

scissors
tagboard

Directions:

1. Draw a tree shape on the poster board.
2. Have a child use the triangular sponge and green paint to sponge-paint the tree. Allow the paint to dry.
3. Have the child use the circular sponge and various colors of paint to make ornament prints on the tree.
4. Cut out the tree, dividing it into two pieces.
5. Glue strands of tinsel to the base of the tree as shown.
6. Add a tagboard headband to each tree's top.
7. Add a strip of heavy tape to the top of the tree's bottom; then punch four holes near its top where indicated.
8. Lace yarn through the holes as shown, leaving enough length for tying the ends.

Sheli Gossett—Gr. K, Avon
Elementary School, Avon
Park, FL

Paper-Chain Tree

This crafty Christmas tree gets your class-room decorated for the holiday and displays the paper ornaments your students make! In advance, cut a large supply of green bulletin board paper strips. Demonstrate for students how to use the strips and glue to make a paper chain. Then have each child make a long chain. (Make sure each chain is the same length and will reach from ceiling to floor.) Attach one end of each chain to a 12-inch embroidery hoop. Then use fishing line to hang the hoop from the ceiling. Attach the opposite end of each chain to a Hula-Hoop toy positioned on the floor. If desired, tape garland to the hoops as shown to disguise them. Attach paper ornaments made by students using tape, glue, or staples. Beautiful!

Rachel R. Pasichow—PreK–Gr.1
P. S. 235 Early Childhood Center, Brooklyn, NY

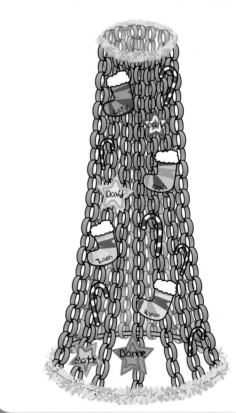

Santa Snack

Four ingredients is all you'll need for this kid-friendly recipe! After checking for peanut allergies, purchase Nutter Butter cookies, vanilla frosting, M&M's Minis candies, and mini white chocolate chips. Tint half of the frosting with red food coloring. Gather a paper plate and plastic knife for each child. Arrange the ingredients and supplies for easy student access. Have each youngster spread half his cookie with white frosting and the other half with red frosting. Instruct him to add three M&M's Minis candies for his Santa's eyes and nose. Then have him add a mini white chocolate chip to the red half to represent the pom-pom on Santa's hat. Your youngsters are sure to have a ho-ho-whole lot of fun decorating these cookies!

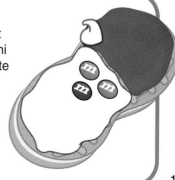

Handprint Kinara

These *kinaras* will be as unique as your students because they are made with their handprints! To prepare, gather brown, red, black, green, and yellow paint; paint brushes; and a 9" x 12" sheet of white construction paper for each child. Fold each sheet of construction paper in half. Working with one child at a time, paint his left palm and four fingers with a generous amount of brown paint. Help him position his hand on the paper so that his index finger makes a print along the fold. Refold the paper to transfer the print to the other side; then unfold it. Next, paint his finger with a generous amount of red, black, or green paint and help him make prints for candles as shown. Finally, instruct him to dip his finger in yellow paint and make a print at the top of each candle to represent the flame. Wow, these *kinaras* are bright, beautiful, and unique!

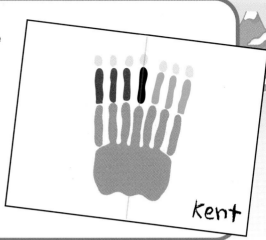

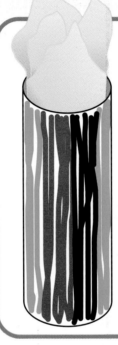

Crafty Candles

Your students will love making these special candle crafts, especially when they learn that a treat for them has been placed inside! In advance, collect a class supply of toilet paper tubes. Provide each child with a 4½" x 6½" piece of paper and red, black, and green markers or crayons. Instruct her to color her entire paper, creating a pattern with the three colors. Tape her patterned paper around a tube. To make the flame, place a small treat in the center of a 12-inch piece of yellow tissue paper. Gather the corners of the tissue and twist the ends together. Slip the flame into the tube so that the twisted end sticks out of the top. All done!

Harvest Snack

Your little ones will be eager to make one of these sweet corn treats for Kwanzaa! First, check for peanut allergies. Gather the ingredients, utensils, and supplies listed below. Then help each child follow the directions to make his own harvest snack.

Ingredients needed for one snack:
Nutter Butter cookie
vanilla frosting tinted yellow
2 leaf-shaped pieces of green Fruit Roll-Ups snacks

Utensils and supplies per child:
paper plate
plastic knife

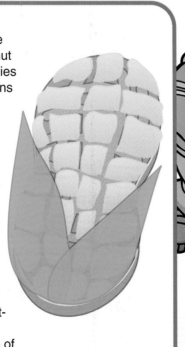

Directions:
1. Spread a cookie with frosting.
2. Use your knife to score the frosting in a grid pattern to look like corn kernels.
3. Put a piece of Fruit Roll-Up snack on each side of the cookie to represent the corn husks.